Teresa's Bible studies are some of the best [...]
a way to teach biblical truth with profoun[...]
winsome and relatable way. This resource is a treasure!

KAT ARMSTRONG, author of *No More Holding Back* and *The In-Between Place*

Teresa, my pink-haired theologian, I want to hug you for writing these studies. You have shared practical, personal, and challenging ways to make the Bible come alive. When a smart woman chases after the heart of God, we all win.

TRICIA LOTT WILLIFORD, author of *You Can Do This* and *Just. You. Wait.*

In a noisy world filled with opinion, it can be difficult to cut through the clutter to find the voice of God and His vision for our lives. Plus, let's face it . . . the Bible is both intriguing and, at the same time, intimidating. Teresa does a beautiful job of taking us into God's heart by walking us through His Word. Her guided studies are for any woman who is wrestling with a sense of direction and believing in her worth. By taking us through the Scriptures in a practical, personal, and powerful way, she equips us to own our *now* and step boldly into our *next*.

MARSHAWN EVANS DANIELS, Godfidence Coach, TV personality, reinvention strategist for women, founder of SheProfits.com

With a relatable voice, Teresa makes studying the Bible approachable for women at any stage of faith. The Get Wisdom Bible Studies are a 360-degree look at God's Word with historical contexts, word studies, hands-on application, and commentary for each day's devotion. The studies are timely with varied messages of practicing contentment, trusting God in hard times, and leading the next generation. Teresa is serious about knowing God and how His character changes His people—the reader is not only encouraged to learn but to *live* the truths in these Bible studies.

BAILEY T. HURLEY, author, blogger, and speaker

Get ready for a Bible study that breaks the mold. Self-proclaimed "Bible nerd" Teresa Swanstrom Anderson has a passion for Scripture that is contagious. But don't you dare think this is a nerdy approach to study. Her warm and approachable style feels like a conversation with a wise and humble friend. Along the way, she will challenge you to *pick up your Bible* as she weaves linguistics, history lessons, and personal stories around a passage. I can't wait to recommend this series to women in our church.

GREG HOLDER, lead pastor at The Crossing; author of *The Genius of One* and *Never Settle*

GET WISDOM BIBLE STUDIES

Living for What Really Matters

7 Weeks in the Book of *Philippians*

NavPress

A NavPress resource published in alliance
with Tyndale House Publishers

NavPress is the publishing ministry of The Navigators, an international Christian organization and leader in personal spiritual development. NavPress is committed to helping people grow spiritually and enjoy lives of meaning and hope through personal and group resources that are biblically rooted, culturally relevant, and highly practical.

For more information, visit NavPress.com.

Visit the author online at teresaswanstromanderson.com.

For all women who are willing to live differently.

Let's step into authenticity and community,
while lavishing love on others . . . because we're
all messy and yet Christ loves us anyway.

Let's Connect

Take a few moments to be replenished . . .
so that you can pour into others.

 teresaswanstromanderson.com

 @teresa.swanstrom.anderson

 GetWisdomBibleStudies.com

I can't wait to discover all God is doing to help you pursue a life that really matters though this study in Philippians. I'd love to see and read all about it! Post using the hashtag #livingforwhatreallymatters on Instagram, Twitter, and/or Facebook so we can encourage one another as we go through this study.

Teresa

Get to know Teresa

Teresa Swanstrom Anderson is a blogger, author, speaker, and Bible study teacher. Teresa grew up in Seattle, but spent her middle school years in Guatemala and has a deep love for people in developing countries. Now living in Denver, Colorado, with her husband and six children, she spends her days wiping off sticky counters, Instagramming, and blogging at teresaswanstromanderson.com. She is the author of *Beautifully Interrupted* and has published several Bible studies on her blog. The Get Wisdom Bible Studies are her first traditionally published studies, taking her passion for studying the Bible and helping women to a broader audience.

Contents

Introduction

Never walk away from Wisdom—she guards your life;
love her—she keeps her eye on you.
Above all and before all, do this: Get Wisdom!
Write this at the top of your list: Get Understanding!
Throw your arms around her—believe me, you won't regret it;
never let her go—she'll make your life glorious.
She'll garland your life with grace,
she'll festoon your days with beauty.

PROVERBS 4:6-9, MSG

As a society, we not only like instant gratification—we expect it. We have on-demand movies, Netflix, and Hulu. When our favorite artist releases a new album, we download it onto our phones. If we want a new book, we can get it on our Kindle or listen to it on Audible with a single click. Even two-day shipping seems too slow for us sometimes, doesn't it?

But here's the thing: Growing in our relationship with Christ isn't necessarily quick. There is no instant download to encountering God. We can't pull up into the Starbucks drive-through and leave minutes later with a full grasp of the Bible and what it says about God and means for our lives.

So if you want a bullet-points-only, CliffsNotes experience of the Bible, this study may not be for you. But don't let that freak you out! I get that life is busy, and I promise—we *can* engage deeply with God through His Word in the midst of everything we're doing without being overwhelmed.

If you are a woman whose life isn't perfect, who struggles balancing all aspects of life and wearing all the hats—but you have a genuine desire to grow in your relationship with Jesus in intentional ways that don't require hours a day—then welcome! I'm hopping up onto my chair and throwing confetti around because, my dear friend, you're exactly where you're supposed to be. Together we're going to see the pages of the Bible come alive—and see the God of the Bible become more a part of our everyday experience as a result.

WHY WE STUDY THE BIBLE

The last time Jesus showed Himself to His disciples after His resurrection, mere moments before His ascension, something happened that is crucial for us to remember as we approach the Bible together. Luke 24:44-45 says, "Then he said to them, 'These are my words that I spoke to you while I was still with you—that everything written about me in the law of Moses, the prophets, and the psalms must be fulfilled.' Then he opened their minds to understand the scriptures" (NRSV).

We should be encouraged: Jesus opened their minds to understand that everything written about Him in Scripture must be fulfilled—but I am certain this isn't the only time Jesus has given individuals unique understanding.

He may even give it to you.

But here's the thing: These men had heard Scripture all their lives. They were ordinary working-class men without higher education. Not one of them had gone to school to become a rabbi, and they did not own a scroll or Bible. Yet because Scripture was read every time these men went to worship and biblical stories were retold throughout their lives, this knowledge was deep within the recesses of their minds and hearts. From childhood, these disciples heard God's Word.

We can know something, however, without understanding it. And that's where the disciples were operating from.

Jesus decided to use this moment before His ascension to turn the spigot, and all their previous knowledge, the buildup of years of knowing God's Word, poured out. Except now, with Jesus' hand on that faucet, everything they had learned and heard through the years suddenly made sense to them.

With the help of Jesus, knowledge was finally tied together with comprehension, and the disciples had a major aha moment.

Just like the disciples, we won't have aha moments every time we open the Bible, worship, or pray. We will have days or even weeks when we don't "feel" any big revelations or hear whispered promptings from the Lord.

Do you feel like you're reading the Bible wrong or even wasting your time without having those heartfelt or aha moments? If you're like me, you want those heart moments all the time. That's when we feel especially close to Jesus. But here's the thing . . . it's not about us. Reading the Bible is not about having God give us a warm fuzzy feeling. It's not to show us how to act and react; neither is it about Him speaking to us. Spending time in the Word is about learning who God is. It's about growing in knowledge of the Creator of the universe and our Lord and Savior. Period.

When I realized a few years ago that the Word of God is not about me but about Him, I was rocked. I realized every verse within every page is written with the intent of us learning more about God's character and love.

Every story, every illustration, and every law loops back around to teach us who He is.

The Bible obviously shares how we should live and who we should be as lovers of the Lord, but it does so in relation to who God is and how He views us. That's why, whether you've loved Christ for five minutes or five decades, I'm just thrilled to be walking through this study of God's Word with you. Together we get to learn more about who He is! As we continue spending time with Him both in the

Word and in prayer, we'll be more prepared to experience Him when He opens our minds like He did for the disciples.

BEFORE WE BEGIN

The Bible

When I was young, I loved collecting. Specifically, I collected bottle caps and napkins. It's okay, you can laugh—it's totally weird. I had boxes of party napkins. I just loved that they were all different, like little pieces of art. Looking back, it kind of makes sense—I love entertaining and setting a pretty table. I still collect those fun napkins so I'm always ready when someone comes over, but I've also begun to collect something else: Bibles.

Why Bibles? Well, the two-hundred-year-old ones passed down from my grandfather are admittedly pieces of art, but I also have shelves of current versions. Still scratching your head as to why I'd have more than one? Well, let me tell you: because different versions say things in different ways.

A great way of understanding Scripture is consulting various translations. Though these Bibles may be worded differently, they don't ultimately differ in meaning and intent, because they all come from the Greek and Hebrew languages the Bible was originally written in.

Some translations are more literal in interpretation than others, however. For example, both *The Message* (MSG) and The Voice translation (VOICE) capture the tone and essence of the text, while the New Revised Standard Version (NRSV), English Standard Version (ESV), and Amplified Bible (AMP) translations are known to be more literal, emphasizing word-for-word accuracy, literary excellence, and depth of meaning. In other words, versions like *The Message* should be looked at as a reading Bible (almost like a commentary that illuminates the text), rather than as a literal Bible, which is better for deep study.

Don't feel like you need to be a crazy Bible-lady like me, with shelves full of varying translations. The great thing about the internet is you can simply find different versions online. I encourage you to download the Bible Gateway or YouVersion app on your phone or head to their sites on your laptop. Try out a few different versions, and see which ones resonate with you best. If you have a favorite Bible already, google what the Bible you're using is translated for. Is it written for tone and intended meaning? Or is it translated for literal, word-for-word interpretation? Is it a reading Bible or a studying Bible?

In many weeks of this study, we'll explore a reading version of the passage, such as *The Message*, *The Voice*, or *The Passion Translation*, which will help us grasp the thematic picture in more accessible language. As we break apart each passage and dive in deeper, we will use the literal translations, so make sure you have one at the ready. I'll include the text from *The Message*, but in most cases, you will need to reference your own Bible or the Bible app on your phone for the rest. Make sense? Great!

Commentaries and Resources

If we want to be bold women who love God deeply, we must be women of Scripture. We must love the Bible in a way that surpasses others' opinion and research. To become spiritually literate, we must become a student of the Word. Commentaries and books about the Bible are incredibly helpful, but we need to make sure we're not spending more time in books *about* the Bible than in the *actual* Bible.

To be clear, I'm not saying we shouldn't refer to sermons and use commentaries. It would be foolish not to take advantage of the wisdom of others whom we have deep respect for. God has most certainly given the gift of discernment in regards to unraveling the Scripture to unique individuals.

I often study with a commentary or two nearby (in fact, I currently have three opened here on my desk),[1] but through the years, I've learned how important it is to make my own interpretation and have my own thoughts about a Scripture passage (even if it's mostly questions) before considering someone else's thoughts and interpretation. I need to make sure my first Guide is God, rather than humans.

The first thing I'd like us to do is turn to a resource that can help us wrestle with what we're actually reading in the Bible. As we sort through God's Word, we need to be curious about the meanings beyond simply our initial understanding. That's why, in addition to adding the Bible Gateway or YouVersion app onto your phone, I'd also like you to download the Blue Letter Bible (BLB). This is really important because we're going to reference it All. The. Time.

All of these apps I'm recommending are free, but if you want to download only one, choose the BLB because it has Bible translation options in addition to lots of extra resources. We'll be using this app every day in this study because it allows us to easily dig into the languages of the Bible (the Hebrew and Aramaic, the languages in which the Old Testament was written, and Greek, the New Testament's language).

If your eyes are glazing over and you're beginning to rethink wanting to do our study because "Whaaat? Dissecting Greek and Hebrew sounds hard / boring / not for me"—I get it. But this is something you can do! And digging into the Bible on this level is how we learn to study for ourselves and not have a faith that is spoon-fed to us. We want to make sure we are learning God's truth, right? Not just someone else's thoughts!

The BLB will rock your world if you haven't used it before. It totally changed the way I study. I'll show you really quickly how it can do the same for you. First, let's open the app and click on the search icon at the top. Let's look up something random like Psalm 23. (By the way, depending on whether you're in the app or on the website, you may want to choose a different Bible translation that better aligns with the wording we're discussing in the study—the BLB has a few different options.) Read verse 1 and see what questions come to mind. *Hmmm . . . what does it mean,* I shall not want? *Like, I'll literally never want for anything if the Lord is my Shepherd?*

Now this is the fun part. We can figure out what these words mean in the original language so we can better comprehend what God wants us to understand! To get there, tap the number by verse 1. On the screen that pops up, tap on *Interlinear** (we'll be using this function a lot!). On the next screen, scroll down to the phrase or word that you're wanting to dig into—in this case, *I shall not want.* You'll see that in the Hebrew the word is חָסֵר or *chacer*. What does that word mean? Go ahead and click on it to find out.

On the page that pops up, you'll find all sorts of information about this word: how to say it, what part of speech it is, what its synonyms are. My favorite sections on this page are *Strong's Definitions* and the *Gesenius' Hebrew-Chaldee Lexicon.*

Now, let's say that learning more about the word and its meaning didn't clear up our question. We've started to dig in ourselves and not simply accept someone else's explanation of a biblical passage—but since things are still a little unclear, let's head to the commentaries.

Navigate back to Psalm 23 and click on verse 1 again. This time, click on the *Text Commentaries* option. Some of my favorites in the app are by Matthew Henry and C. H. Spurgeon, but look through all of them to find which ones are most helpful to you. For the purposes of our exploration, let's tap on Spurgeon's Psalm 23 commentary. Here's my takeaway from what he wrote: "I shall not want" means I may not possess all that I wish for, but I am given a spirit of contentment. After all, does God not feed the ravens and cause the lilies to grow? I know that His grace will be sufficient for me.

Other places where you can find cross-references, commentaries, and lexicons online are Bible Hub (biblehub.com) and Bible Study Tools (biblestudytools.com). So many discoveries and insights are just a click away! When you start researching word, context, and commentaries in your study of the Bible, that is often the beginning of more questions and jumping down bunny trails of more questions

---

* On iPhones, this is called *Interlinear/Concordance*; to get to this function on the website, click on *Tools* next to the verse first.

and research. But you know what? The point of spending time in the Bible isn't to check off a task and move on with our day. Second Peter 3:18 says, "But grow in the grace and knowledge of our Lord and Savior Jesus Christ. To him be the glory both now and to the day of eternity."

Spending time in the Word and with the Lord is about gaining wisdom and knowledge. So if you decide to bounce around even more than I do within these pages and go down bunny trails that I have yet to discover, do it! You can spend fifteen minutes on a passage of Scripture or fifteen days, months, or years. This is all for you and your relationship with Him!

HOW TO USE THIS STUDY

Who + How

There are several ways you can engage in this study. Here are some tips for each context:

1. *Individually*: If you're doing this on your own, that's great! Write in the margins, highlight sections where God seems to want to get your attention, star things, put big question marks in areas you'd like to dig into further. Get this book messy! This study is a conversation between you and the Lord, so freewrite throughout as you really dig into all the beautiful things He wants to chat with you about!

2. *One-on-One*: We grow most in community, so find a friend who would like to do the study with you! Perhaps you'll meet together every week over coffee or lunch. Or maybe you'll meet over the phone or virtually.

3. *In-Person Group*: If you are doing this study in a group setting, such as a church Bible study or home group, still strive to be 100 percent honest and authentic in your answers. Often,

when we're with other women, we're afraid that they might judge our struggles, anger, pain, or even questions we have for or about God. But when we hide our true selves, we won't see the spiritual, emotional, and relational growth that can come out of time with other people who love Jesus. Of course, if the conversation dives into particular sections or questions that you don't feel ready to share publicly, give yourself permission to not answer. But if the group feels safe and supportive, I encourage you to bring all of yourself—including your messiness. And remember—even when you're in a group, make sure to invest in your daily, personal study! Coming to the group time after careful engagement with the Scripture will help everyone flourish.

For more specific directions on how to use this study as a group, head to GetWisdomBibleStudies.com to download the PDF guide. This guide will map out how to use this resource in an eight-week study and how to focus on questions and themes most beneficial for group discussion, as well as how to create and facilitate a healthy group.

4. *Virtual Group*: If you're not plugged into a group in your local context, why not start your own virtual group via Zoom, FaceTime, Skype, or another video-conference website and app? Or perhaps your friends are super busy and spread across the state or country (or world!), so finding an actual day and time to meet proves difficult. If this is the case, you can start your own Facebook group, decide who will facilitate, and start chatting about what you're learning each day or each week. You and your friends can simply post whenever works best for everyone's individual schedules! Sounds fun, right?

Each day of this study can take you only twenty to thirty minutes, but if you'd like to dig deeper, you'll be learning the skills to explore more deeply in the passage of Scripture and the context of Paul's letter to the Philippians. At the end of each day, you'll be prompted into a time of journaling prayer, so you can talk to and hear from God as He draws you more deeply into a life that really matters.

When + Where

Before starting this study, consider when in your day would best provide some uninterrupted time to dig in. I know finding time can be so difficult in our busy lives, thanks to jobs, kids, and other responsibilities. But we make time for the things that matter—and I promise, time meeting God through His Word is so worth it.

Personally, though I'm certainly not a morning person (hello, coffee), my brain is most attentive in the morning . . . plus, I really love having time with the Lord to center myself before the chaos of the day begins. Through the years, my family notices when I haven't done this for a few days—my joy, patience, and kindness just isn't what it usually is when I'm in the Word at the start of the day!

Simply can't get up any earlier than you currently do? Maybe you work shifts or have little ones not yet sleeping all the way through the night. I get it, and I've been there. I still encourage you to give God the firstfruits of your time, though. Throughout the Bible, we are encouraged to give the first and best to the Lord. And though we may not have a first crop of corn or a perfect lamb to present to Him, we certainly can give Him the first of our time—not the leftovers. Even if rising earlier in the morning feels impossible in this season, you can still offer Him your firstfruits. Pack a bag with your Bible and this study and do it at the beginning of your lunch hour at work, first break between classes, or the first moments of your child's naptime. The laundry, dishes, and showering can wait. Put Him first.

What You'll Need

This study is meant both to guide you through the book of Philippians and to equip you to forge your own path through God's Word so He can make it alive in your everyday life. As you begin your study, here are a few things to keep on hand:

- A Bible in your favorite translation
- Your phone with the Blue Letter Bible app and BibleGateway or YouVersion downloaded
- A pen (you'll find space to write as we explore the book of Philippians together, but also feel free to scribble in the margins as you need to!)
- A smartphone with internet access so you can watch the short videos that introduce each week (you can find those at GetWisdomBibleStudies.com).
- A place without distraction where you can truly dig in!

One Last Thing

A final note to remember as we go through this study: The Bible was written for us, but it's not written *to* us. The Bible is full of stories, poetry, laws, parables, and such, which were written for people who lived in a different culture thousands of years before any of us were born. So each week in this study, we're going to explore some of the behind-the-scenes aspects of Scripture. We're going to figure out the historical and cultural background. We'll try to learn the *why* of it all.

We need to become not just readers of the Word . . . but *studiers* of it. Only then can we understand what God has *for* us in His Word.

LIVING FOR WHAT REALLY MATTERS

What do our lives say about what we think really matters? We glorify busyness—and yet we also acknowledge that hustle leads to burnout. Our mantras are "progress, not perfection" and "my current situation is not my final destination," yet we feel hopeless and pessimistic when life isn't "how it should be."

But what if it's only *pointless* hustle that leads to burnout? What if struggle can be valuable if we allow it to lead us to growth and depth? What if trading "likes" and approval for authenticity leads to joy?

Philippians is often referred to as the "joy book" of the Bible—and though it's true that Paul speaks eloquently about joy throughout, we can miss the powerful statement he's making about life in Christ if we focus on joy alone. This book is not just about joy manufactured out of nowhere: It is, most profoundly, about the fundamental reality of what it means to live for Jesus among the people of Jesus. It's about unity and community, authenticity and dependence on God no matter the season . . . and out of that, deep and meaningful joy. This—not success, not achievement, not independence, not comfort—is the life that really matters.

As we journey together through the book of Philippians, let's learn how to intentionally develop lives that make a difference—by growing deep roots in community and blossoming in the midst of whatever we face.

Let's get to it!

Take joy,

Living in Authenticity

Philippians 1:1-11

WEEK 1 • *Day 1*

 READ ACTS 9

I used to write out exactly what I was going to say when I broke up with someone. One time in college, I wrote and rewrote my break-up monologue for an entire week straight. I penned it during every class, every study break, and any other time I had a few minutes to myself. I had a *really* hard time telling people what needed to be said.

Our buddy Paul, though? Not so much.

In the book of Philippians, Paul has some hard conversations with the church in Philippi. He says what needs to be said, encourages what needs encouragement, and corrects what need correcting. Paul doesn't sugarcoat anything.

My husband is this way. He's always quick to tell me when I hurt his feelings or if my tone with the kids was harsher than I'd intended. He gives me ideas on how I can lead more effectively, and he's up front when he needs more us-time. Maybe that's why I like Paul so much. After years of living with someone who gives it to me straight, I understand the importance of real, authentic conversation. Sometimes these kinds of conversations are empowering. Sometimes they're not super fun. But since Ben's words are coming from a place of love, I know they're not meant to harm. We meet in authenticity to help each other grow. Sweeping things under the rug or being passive-aggressive isn't beneficial or healthy.

If we want to be bold, dynamic women of God, we need to be willing to fight for authenticity in community. We have one life to live—one shot to make a mark on this earth in the name of Jesus Christ. And with Paul as our teacher, we'll learn how to do that.

But if we're going to learn from Paul, we need to first understand a bit more about who this man is. Now, I do realize you may know Paul's backstory already, but as we walk through it again, God may point something out to you that somehow reflects and refracts differently today. God likes to highlight things at certain times, as He wants you to know, learn, and grow.

In Acts, we learn that Saul (Paul's original Hebrew name) hated those who believed that Jesus was the Messiah. If we look at Philippians 3:5, we can get a sense why he felt this way: Not only was he from a Jewish family, but he was a devout and legalistic Pharisee. This new faith seemed like heresy to him.

1. What does Acts 9:1-2 say about Saul?

Saul's conversion is incredible. God intervenes in a dramatic and supernatural way—and He steps into the path of someone no one thought would ever become a Christian.

Do you know someone like that? A person you've been praying for, and yet it just seems so unlikely that they'd turn from their current lifestyle and become a new creation? But the beginning of Paul's story tells us something extraordinary: We serve a limitless God who often does the unlikely.

 ### History Lesson

We know that God changed Abram's name to Abraham (Genesis 17:5), Sarai to Sarah (Genesis 17:15), and Jacob to Israel (Genesis 32:28). And most of us probably thought God did the same to Saul, whom we know as Paul in the New Testament. But is that really what happened? Let's find out.

- When Jesus speaks to him on the road to Damascus, he addresses him as Saul: "Saul, Saul, why are you persecuting me?" (Acts 9:4).

- When Ananias speaks to him after his conversion, he also calls him Saul: "Brother Saul, the Lord Jesus who appeared to you on the road by which you came has sent me so that you may regain your sight and be filled with the Holy Spirit" (Acts 9:17).

- When Paul was called out before his first missionary trip, the Holy Spirit refers to him as Saul: "Set apart for me Barnabas and Saul for the work to which I have called them" (Acts 13:2).

In fact, after his conversion, Paul is referred to as Saul fourteen times![1] Hmm. So . . . what's the deal? Why did his name change?

The shift from Saul to Paul happens as he sets sail for his missionary journeys. In Acts 13:9, we see Saul is called "Paul" for the first time on the island of Cyprus, which is much later than his conversion. Luke, the author of Acts, indicates in this verse that these two names are interchangeable: "But Saul, who was also called Paul, filled with the Holy Spirit, looked intently at him."

Saul was the Hebrew form of his name; Paul was the Roman form. He uses the name Paul as he continues to travel and share the Good News of Jesus to mostly non-Jewish individuals throughout the Mediterranean. The shift in names is a sign of Paul's desire to be approachable in the way he shared the gospel, using language and even his name in a way unique audiences could relate to (see 1 Corinthians 9:19-23).[2]

In Acts 9:10-11, we see God ask a man named Ananias to do something that seemed crazy: to go meet up with Saul. Ananias knows of this man named Saul of Tarsus and all the horrible things he's been a part of in and around Jerusalem. In fact, the first time we hear Saul's name in the Bible is during the stoning of Stephen, the first Christian martyr:

> Then they cast him out of the city and stoned him. And the witnesses laid down their garments at the feet of a young man named Saul.
> ACTS 7:58

Can you imagine being asked to meet with this kind of man? Ananias probably felt like he was being asked to go to his death!

2. How does Ananias initially respond to God?

_____

_____

_____

3. How does the Lord reply to Ananias' concern? (Hint: See verses 15-16.)

_____

_____

_____

_____

God knows something Ananias doesn't: The man who had spent so much time persecuting Christians is now a completely new person.

4. Flip over to 2 Corinthians 5:17. What happens when we follow Jesus?

_____

_____

_____

_____

You can make yourself better, but only Christ can make you new. And if ever there was someone who became a new creation, it was Paul.

So what exactly does *new* mean, anyway? Let's go to the BLB app to find out. Head to 2 Corinthians 5 and click on verse 17. Tap on the *Interlinear* and scroll down to find the word *new* or *kainos* (καινός, pronounced *kai-nos*).† Click on the word to find English synonyms and descriptions from *Outline of Biblical Usage*, *Strong's Definitions*, and *Thayer's Greek Lexicon*, as well as all the other New Testament verses that use *kainos*.

5. Pen down what *kainos* means:

_____

_____

_____

_____

_____

I absolutely love how *Thayer's Greek Lexicon* explains this word: "recently made, fresh, recent, unused, unworn."[3] So often as Christians, we talk about being restored . . . but this verse reveals that we're *more* than restored. Restored would mean we're just a new-and-improved version of what we were before. But this verse here in 2 Corinthians tells us that no matter what we've done or how we've lived, in Christ, we are *brand new*.

What does that tell us about Paul? When he chose to follow Jesus, his history against the church was wiped out, wiped clean. It doesn't mean there weren't consequences (like having to build trust and demonstrate the authenticity of his newness to Ananias and a multitude of believers), but in God's eyes, there is no *before*—there is only *now* and *evermore*.

---

† In random order, the theme of these answers are: *declares his confidence in God, complains of his circumstances, sings praise to God, lifts his heart in prayer.*

6. If Paul was made completely new the moment he chose to follow Jesus, why do you think Jesus blinded Paul? Just share your best guess.

_____

_____

_____

_____

Paul's blindness could only be explained as an encounter with Jesus Christ Himself. And being blind allowed Paul to live undistracted for several days. He likely played and replayed the experience in his head and reflected on all his years of misunderstanding what it meant to truly love and follow God. But I don't think that's all. I wonder if Jesus was using literal blindness to show Paul that he had been living a life of spiritual blindness. As Paul's sight was restored, so was his relationship with Jesus and his understanding of his new life with the Creator of the universe.

 ### *History Lesson*

The New Testament is comprised of twenty-seven books, thirteen of which are attributed to Paul. Additionally, about half of the book of Acts (written by Luke) is filled with stories of Paul's life and works. Scholars debate whether Paul also wrote Hebrews. If he did, he would have contributed fourteen books (or 51.85 percent of the entire New Testament!). Of these epistles, only seven are accepted as "being entirely authentic and dictated by St. Paul himself." The others are thought to have been written by others on behalf of this dynamic apostle.[4] Paul was obviously influential in spreading the gospel in the days of the early church.

DATE	EPISTLE	CONTEXT
AD 52–53	1 and 2 Thessalonians	after second missionary journey began
AD 57–58	1 and 2 Corinthians, Galatians, and Romans	after third missionary journey began
AD 62	Ephesians, Philemon, Colossians, and Philippians	during Paul's first Roman imprisonment
AD 63	1 Timothy and Titus	after being acquitted
AD 66	2 Timothy	during Paul's second Roman imprisonment

As we consider Paul's "newness"—and by extension, the being-made-new that each of us experiences when we follow Jesus—we might find ourselves wondering how this utter transformation happens. Look again at Acts 9:15. God told Ananias, "He [Paul] is a chosen instrument of mine." When I look at this verse in the *Interlinear* section of the BLB, I see that *instrument* (*skeuos*; σκεῦος, pronounced *skyoo-os*) also means "vessel."⁵ Like the white geometric vase on my desk, which is filled with beautiful flowers, a vessel *contains* something. Is *filled* with something. God hand-selected this vessel (Paul) that once contained judgment and pharisaical law, removed his spiritual blindness, and made him new . . . and now the vessel is filled with the Holy Spirit. We know from Galatians that as we are filled with the Holy Spirit, we pour out the fruit of the Spirit—which is the very character of God.

7. What fruit of the Spirit might you expect to see emerge in Paul's writings? (Hint: See Galatians 5:22-23.)

The book of Philippians gives us a vivid picture of the fruit of the Spirit, as Paul writes to his Philippian friends about living aligned with the Good News of Jesus: love, not legalism; unity, not discord; authentic faith, not counterfeit religion.

When Paul's eyesight returned, he saw the world with new eyes because he truly was a new creation. Gentiles (non-Jews) that he once despised and looked down on became his friends. The body of Christ (the early church) that he once persecuted became his family. Nothing was the same after his encounter with Jesus. Sharing the gospel of Jesus Christ became his only goal, and he willingly left the safety of his old life to share the Good News with the world. Three missionary journeys took him through areas of the globe where people had yet to hear the name of Jesus, and he faced almost constant danger:

> ^{25} Three times I was beaten with rods. Once I was stoned. Three times I was shipwrecked; a night and a day I was adrift at sea; ^{26} on frequent journeys, in danger from rivers, danger from robbers, danger from my own people, danger from Gentiles, danger in the city, danger in the wilderness, danger at sea, danger from false brothers; ^{27} in toil and hardship, through many a sleepless night, in hunger and thirst, often without food, in cold and exposure.
>
> 2 CORINTHIANS 11:25-27

If we flip back over to Acts 9:16, we see that God let Ananias in on what lay in store for this murderer-turned-apostle. The Lord knew that Paul would suffer "for the sake of [His] name." Yet, because Paul-made-new was filled with love, joy, peace, patience, kindness, goodness, faithfulness, gentleness, and self-control, he could see God's deeper purpose in every struggle. The struggle was not beyond the reach of God, and every bit of pain was worth God's Kingdom reaching the ends of the earth.

I'm sure Paul sometimes felt unqualified and inadequate in the face of such a difficult calling. But you know what? When we feel unqualified and inadequate, we can fully lean on the One who *is* able to do all things.

This is important for us to realize: If we feel capable and qualified for God's task, we're probably leaning on our own power and ability instead of God's, which means we're either out of step with what He's asking or we're about to struggle mightily in pursuit of the calling.

8. Do you feel capable and qualified in your calling? Where have you gotten comfortable, and do you think you might be missing something more that God is calling you to?

God qualifies the called; He doesn't call the qualified. That's certainly true of Paul. He had participated in persecution and murder of God's people. I'm sure he often felt massively over his head as he faced persecution and prison.

But guess what—being over our heads is a *good* thing. If we're living in self-reliance and self-sufficiency, we've made ourselves god. God wants us to join Him in His Kingdom work, and to be up to that task, we have to recognize our insufficiency and lean on His ultimate sufficiency.

God doesn't want us to simply *look* the part of a new creation—He wants us to *be* a new creation. This newness equals freedom in Him. And freedom in Him creates opportunity. How do we make the most of this freedom and opportunity? We give our whole self to Him. We open our hands and give our all to Him. We say the words "send me"—even before we understand where and how we will be sent. This is the only way we are qualified: as vessels filled with the Holy Spirit.

Paul's life was so radically changed after his encounter with Jesus that his entire existence became about sharing the redeeming love of the Cross. Paul cared little about who others thought he *should* be, or about what he "gave up" in choosing to follow Jesus. Instead, Paul leaned into authentic truth, integrity, and unity. I love what John Piper says about Paul:

> He does not need my approval. He doesn't fear my rejection. He does not have his finger in the air to discern how the winds of culture are blowing. He is authentic.[6]

Isn't this the type of woman we want to be? I don't want to do things simply for the approval of others. I don't want to fear rejection or internet trolls. I don't want to change my stance or my direction with the winds of culture. I want to be authentic and live in authentic relationships with others. And I have a feeling you do too.

Spend some time in prayer, talking to God about places in your life where you struggle to live authentically. Ask Him to give you the trust and freedom to live wholly in who He has created you to be.

Amen.

READ ACTS 16:6-40

I love seeing women of God making a difference for the Kingdom of God. And our heavenly Father does too. That's why I was delighted when I realized that the Philippian church existed in part because of several women who fell in love with Jesus. They hadn't met Jesus, and they hadn't yet met Paul, but the Good News about Jesus had spread to their city—and their hearts responded.

Even before he met the women of Philippi, Paul saw women as valuable partners in the gospel. Did you know that the first convert in Europe was a woman who founded the first European Christian church with Paul?[7] (We'll hear more about Lydia in a bit.) Women weren't included within the twelve disciples because these twelve were to signify the twelve tribes of Israel, but on the day of Pentecost (when the Holy Spirit was poured out), God showed the world that He was doing something even bigger, empowering both men and women to spread the name of Jesus Christ:

> I will pour out my Spirit
>   on every kind of people:
> Your sons will prophesy,
>   also your daughters;
> Your young men will see visions,
>   your old men dream dreams.
> When the time comes,
>   I'll pour out my Spirit
> On those who serve me, men and women both,
>   and they'll prophesy.

ACTS 2:16-17, MSG

The people who led were men *and* women, converted Jew *and* Gentile, circumcised *and* uncircumcised. We know God loves diversity, and we see that here as a new season unfolds. Nothing was the same as it was before. Everything was new and uncharted.

The New Testament indicates that the gospel radically altered the position of women, elevating them to a partnership with men unparalleled in first-century society. Wherever the gospel went, women were among the first, foremost and most faithful converts. The gospel led them to engage in aspects of Christ's service that went beyond the cultural limitations of the day. As Ben Witherington III observes, "In the post-Easter community we find women assuming a greater variety of roles, some of which . . . would have been forbidden to a Jewish woman (e.g., being a teacher of men in Acts 18:24-6)."[8]

 ### *History Lesson*

Another female leader in the New Testament was Priscilla (she and her husband, Aquila, led a church in Ephesus—and later, another one in Rome). If you read their story in Acts 18, you may have noticed that her name is usually mentioned first. This suggests she is the more noteworthy and prominent leader of the two. Priscilla is even listed first when she and her husband explained theology and doctrine to Apollos in Acts 18:24-26. Paul specifically names this amazing couple on several occasions (Romans 16:3-5; 1 Corinthians 16:19; 2 Timothy 4:19). What an incredible woman Priscilla must have been!

As Paul headed out on his second missionary journey, he planned to take the gospel to Asia. But in Acts 16, we learn that God put a big red light on Paul's plan—because He had bigger and better plans:

> 6-8 They went to Phrygia, and then on through the region of Galatia. Their plan was to turn west into Asia province, but the Holy Spirit blocked that route. So they went to Mysia and tried to go north to Bithynia, but the Spirit of Jesus wouldn't let them go there either. Proceeding on through Mysia, they went down to the seaport Troas.
>
> 9-10 That night Paul had a dream: A Macedonian stood on the far shore and called across the sea, "Come over to Macedonia and help us!" The dream gave Paul his map. We went to work at once getting things ready to cross over to Macedonia. All the pieces had come together. We knew now for sure that God had called us to preach the good news to the Europeans.
>
> ACTS 16:6-10, MSG

Did you notice verse 6 says the Holy Spirit "blocked" that route? The Greek word used here is κωλύω (pronounced *kōlyō*) and literally means "to hinder, prevent, forbid," "to withhold a thing," "to deny or refuse one a thing."[9] I don't know how they understood God was blocking them. Perhaps they weren't allowed entrance, or maybe something in their gut told them not to proceed. Whatever the case, God didn't want them in Asia at this point, and in a vivid dream, He directed Paul somewhere else.

God has certainly blocked my way many times before. In my book *Beautifully Interrupted*, I wrote about how the life I live now is not the one I thought I wanted. My plan was to get a doctorate in art history, move to Europe, work as a curator at some fantastic museum . . . and kids? They weren't in my five-year, ten-year, or really *any*-year plan.

But one day I realized I'd never consulted God in any of my plans. As the tattoo on my right wrist now reminds me, I prayed the words "send me." I wish God had told me exactly where to go—but instead of knowing what to do, I almost immediately knew what I *wasn't* supposed to do. And that was continue pursuing art history. He most certainly blocked and forbade that route for me because He had something bigger and more exciting. I see that now, looking back. But at the time, I didn't obey without dragging my feet.

1. Has God ever blocked the path you were going down? What happened? How did you respond?

As we continue reading, we learn that Paul and his travel buddies sailed for Samothrace, then on to Neapolis, and from there, they hoofed it to Philippi. *The Message* says Philippi was "the main city in that part of Macedonia and, even more importantly, a Roman colony," and that they "lingered there several days" (Acts 16:11-12).

On the day of Sabbath, Paul and his companions sought a place to worship. They heard about a prayer meeting held along the riverside, and so they found it and began to speak to the women who had gathered there.

2. Why do you think Paul and his companions didn't go to a synagogue to pray and worship?

To find our answer to this question, we'll need to back up and learn a little about the city itself.

 History Lesson

When they were attacked by Thracians, the inhabitants of this city, previously known as Krenides, sought protection from Philip II of Macedon (the father of Alexander the Great!). Knowing the land was rich in gold, Philip responded by capturing the city himself circa 357 BCE (so much for looking to Philip for help!) and renamed it Philippi.

Years later, after Mark Antony and Octavian took revenge on Julius Caesar's assassins, Brutus and Cassius, Philippi become a military outpost and Roman colony. Because the city teemed with Roman troops, it was often referred to as "little Rome."[10]

Self-governing and independent, Philippi was a bit of a melting pot. Because no synagogue existed, we know that not even ten Jewish males resided within the city limits. But, as Paul and his friends knew, when a city did not have a synagogue, those who loved God would meet by the river to pray and worship.

Lydia was likely a Gentile who had heard of the incredible name of Jesus (John 12:20 shows that news of Jesus' miraculous healings had begun spreading to the people of Greece). She's the only woman named in this passage, so it's likely that although she had never met Jesus and had never been formally taught the gospel, she was leading the meeting.

Isn't it interesting that we don't hear of any men at this prayer meeting, and yet Luke (the author of Acts) says, "We sat down and spoke to the women who had come together" (Acts 16:13)? In those days, Jewish men and women didn't worship together. They even had different sections in the synagogue. Once again, however, we see that tide changing within the community of Jesus followers as men and women come together in their love of Jesus.

3. What do we learn about Lydia in Acts 16:14-15?

 History Lesson

Because Lydia sold "purple goods," her customers would have been the wealthy elite, as extracting this dye took a substantial amount of labor and it was highly valued. Tyrian purple, derived from marine mollusks, was especially costly: extracting this dye involved tens of thousands of snails and was quite arduous. Lydia's hometown of Thyatira was well-known for manufacturing a less expensive and more reddish dye from roots of the madder plant (known today as "Turkey red"). However, since Scripture specifically describes her as a seller of purple (*porphyropōlis*; πορφυρόπωλις, pronounced *por-foo-rop-o-lis*) goods, she was likely selling textiles of the more valuable Tyrian purple.[11]

I love so many things about Lydia and Paul's interaction. She wasted no time telling her entire household everything she learned from Paul as the Lord opened her heart to His wisdom. And *then* she opened her home to Paul and his companions!

Opening my door and inviting people in is something God asked me to do years ago when I was relatively new to Denver and had no friends. Although we were fixing up a previously uninhabitable house at the time, I decided to obey and offer what I had with a thankful heart. I welcomed in anyone I could possibly think of.

Lydia was a successful businesswoman who likely had a large and beautiful home, but that makes her invitation no less meaningful. She knew the importance of creating a space for all to gather. No matter what your environment, your home is *enough* to act as a welcome and safe place for others—and you can open your door too.

As they enjoyed Lydia's warm hospitality, Paul and his three companions frequented the riverside to pray, worship, and teach the gospel. Here they faced a challenge: Day after day, a demon-possessed slave girl followed them around, shouting, "These men are slaves like me, but slaves of the Most High God! They will proclaim to you the way of liberation!" (Acts 16:17, VOICE).

Finally, after many days, the annoyance of her disturbance got the best of Paul, and he cast out the spirit of divination (*pythōn*; πύθων) that lived within her.

 ## History Lesson

The spirit within this slave girl was *python*, a term referring to the mythical snake said to guard the oracle at Delphi. Ancient Greeks believed Delphi to be the center of the world and the term *python* had come to be used of the persons through whom the python guard supposedly spoke and predicted the future.[12]

After Paul cast out the demon, her owners were livid because their fortune-teller would no longer make them money. They seized Paul and Silas and dragged them into the marketplace before the chief leaders of the city.

4. Reread Acts 16:22-24. What happened to Paul and Silas as a result of this situation?

_____

_____

_____

_____

Wait—didn't God direct Paul and his companions to Philippi? Didn't He orchestrate their meeting Lydia and teaching the women at the river, and even healing that poor girl who was a victim of slavery?

Here's the thing we can't forget: *We can be 100 percent following God's will and still go through hard stuff.* Sometimes God's will *takes* us through the hard stuff because He has a purpose in it.

Difficulty brings a rich wisdom that can't be formed elsewhere. If you can have joy in the darkness, you truly understand life with Christ. I'm not saying it's easy. I'm not even saying you'll feel clarity and understanding during every second of hard seasons. But I can promise that clinging to and loving Christ in the midst of even the bleakest situations will develop you into a woman of incredible depth, strength, and empathy.

Think for a moment about the painful circumstances Paul and Silas found themselves in—and the way they chose to respond. Can you imagine being fastened into stocks and still spending hours praying and singing hymns?

I've seen enough movies to understand the concept of stocks. And when I tap on this verse (Acts 16:24) in the BLB app and find the definition in the *Interlinear*, my visualization is confirmed:

> **stocks** (*xylon* or ξύλον, pronounced *ksoo-lon*): "a log or timber with holes in which the feet, hands, neck of prisoners were inserted and fastened with thongs" (strips of leather)[13]

I'm truly not sure how you could breathe, let alone sing, while tortured and bent in this way, yet Paul and Silas did so loudly enough that the guards and prisoners were listening. Everyone around them got to see the depth of their relationship with God, even in the midst of an awful situation. Without God allowing Paul and Silas's imprisonment, these men in the jail would not have learned of the love and light of Jesus in such an incredible way.

5. What happened around midnight? (See Acts 16:25-27.)

6. Why would the guard respond by wanting to kill himself?

The guard knew that he would be tortured to death for his failure to keep the prisoners in their cells, so he decided to kill himself swiftly. But Paul, realizing what was about to happen, shouted that they were all still there.

7. After realizing that the prisoners had not escaped, why do you think the jailer rushed in and asked Paul and Silas what he must do to be saved?

The jailer's entire household was saved and baptized that night. Isn't that incredible? First Lydia (and her household), then the slave girl, and now the jailer (and his family). Paul's plans were diverted, and yet God used every part of his difficulties to bring forth a new community of believers. And as Paul writes this letter to the church in Philippi, though he is again imprisoned, he writes to a church that is firmly rooted and thriving, living for what really matters. All because Paul chose to follow God and thrive no matter what circumstances he faced.

Talk to God about your struggles and pain. Ask Him to open your eyes to what He may be doing through those hard things. God can handle our hurt and even our anger. He wants you to pour out your whole heart to Him.

_____

_____

_____

_____

_____

_____

_____

_____

_____

_____

_____

_____

Amen.

WEEK 1 • *Day 3*

READ PHILIPPIANS 1:1-2

Many years ago, one of my friends sent me a beautiful little book out of the blue: *The Art of the Handwritten Note.*[14] Those delightful pages taught me that the structure of our words means something, and so does the way we open and end a letter. I think Paul would have liked that book. He was all about purposefully placing words in a greeting, his words dripping with power and intentionality.

In the opening of this letter in Philippians 1:1-4, Paul isn't simply greeting the church. Yes, technically that *is* what he's doing, but he's doing so much more than that. Let's look closer. Paul isn't one to waste a single syllable:

> ¹ Paul and Timothy, servants of Christ Jesus,
>   To all the saints in Christ Jesus who are at Philippi, with the overseers and deacons:
>   ² Grace to you and peace from God our Father and the Lord Jesus Christ.
>
> PHILIPPIANS 1:1-2

Head to Philippians 1 in the BLB. Once there, tap on verse 1, and then select *Interlinear*. Scroll down to the term *bond-servants*, and tap on *doulos* (δοῦλος, pronounced *doo-los*).

1. What does the word *bond-servant* mean?

_____

_____

_____

Paul and Timothy aren't held captive by Christ Jesus, working for Him under duress. Paul is saying that they were purchased by Christ for a price—one that He paid on the cross. In the same way, each of us who follows Jesus is now free, slave (to sin) no more. But, while acknowledging that freedom, Paul also uses this word to illustrate his wholehearted commitment to his Master (Jesus). In other words, because of his freedom, he obediently serves.

As we continue, we see Paul refer to the body of believers in Philippi with an interesting term: *saints*.

2. What does this word *saint* make you think of?

_____

_____

_____

When I hear the word *saint*, I'm reminded of my Catholic friends talking about patron saints of things like illnesses, places, or occupations. In fact, Lydia is the patron saint of dyeing because of her purple-dye business mentioned in Acts 16. There's a lot that goes into receiving the title of Saint, not the least of which is that the person needs to be deceased. So Paul is obviously using the word in a different way here. Let's head again to the BLB and find out what he means.

3. Open up the *Interlinear* section of Philippians 1:1. What does this word *saints* (*hagios*; ἅγιος, pronounced *ha-gee-os*) mean?

_____

_____

_____

4. Using what we've learned from the expanded definition of *saints* (*hagios*; ἅγιος), how would you describe them (us)?

_____

_____

_____

 History Lesson

In the early church, the title of *saint* (*hagios*; ἅγιος) was essentially used in the same way the term *Christian* is today. But did you know *Christian* was initially a mocking term?

²⁵ *Barnabas went to Tarsus to look for Saul,* ²⁶ *and when he had found him, he brought him to Antioch. For a whole year they met with the church and taught a great many people. And in Antioch the disciples were first called Christians.*

ACTS 11:25-26

Antioch was a melting pot, referred to as "all the world in one city."[15] Antiochians saw the various Jewish sects as one large group, but the people who followed Jesus were different: Suddenly, Jews and Gentiles were coming together as one people. Quickly seeing the difference between Judaism and Jesus, a different name was needed, so the Antiochians coined the term *little Christs*, or *Christians*. This occurrence in Acts 11 is the first time we read the word *Christians* (*Christianos*; Χριστιανός, pronounced *khrees-tee-a-nos*) in the Bible. It is thought that originally the term was used sneeringly of Jesus followers, like we see in Acts 26:28: "But Agrippa did answer: 'Keep this up much longer and you'll make a Christian out of me!'" (MSG). But the early church claimed the term, happily acknowledging the desire to be little Christs.

In the opening of his letter, Paul wasn't simply acknowledging the *people* of Philippi or even the *body of believers* in Philippi. He was reminding them that they were *sacred*, *holy*, and *consecrated*. Moreover, the Greek word for *saints* in this passage is almost always plural, illustrating that this whole community is set apart for the Lord. This is important, because as Paul moves on to address bishops and deacons, he does so in the context of the larger community. Scripture doesn't share specifically what a bishop or deacon did in the early church, but this leadership wasn't *over* the fellowship of believers. Rather, the bishops and deacons were *part* of the set-apart community. How do we know that? Let's again look at the words Paul used in Philippians 1.

5. Circle the first word in the phrase below:

with the bishops and deacons (NRSV)

With. If we look at that term in the BLB, we discover that the word literally means "including," denoting "togetherness," "union," and "completeness."[16] That doesn't seem much like a hierarchy, does it? Instead, Paul seems to acknowledge that the bishops and deacons are *leading alongside*.

God invented leadership, and He knew the best way forward for the growing church as it spread the gospel: not leadership that placed people *under* but leaders who worked *alongside*.

This was a big deal. God turned the tables on the way things used to be. You see, before Jesus' death and resurrection, and the coming of the Holy Spirit in Acts 2, the only person who had direct access to God was the high priest. A few leaders and prophets were given the gift of personal relationship with God (Moses and Joshua, for example), and in those cases, it was because God Himself had given them a specific task. The normal person—like you and me—didn't have access to God.

But when Jesus died for our sins, the veil that separated the Holy of Holies from the everyday people tore (Matthew 27:51), and God changed everything. He now places us in the company of high priests (1 Peter 2:9) and gives us every privilege and gift of that position.

The leaders of the church in Philippi and the leaders of our churches are on the same playing field as each of us. They are not leading from above, but alongside. No person is higher or more valuable in the eyes of God than anyone else. We can lead people to Christ from wherever we work, live, and stand.

Because of this, leaders of the church need to consider themselves first as a member of the body or community and second as someone who guides. The leaders and the led all make mistakes and sin, we are all saved by grace, and all are wholly and completely dependent on God's mercy and goodness.

Pray for the local church, your community and city, and our nation as a whole to open their hearts to God. Ask the Lord to help us Jesus followers get out of our own way and live in a way that represents Him fully as we pursue the greatest two commandments, which are given by Jesus Himself:

"Love the Lord your God with all your passion and prayer
and intelligence." This is the most important, the first on
any list. But there is a second to set alongside it: "Love
others as well as you love yourself."

MATTHEW 22:37-40, MSG

Amen.

WEEK 1 • *Day 4*

 READ PHILIPPIANS 1:3-8

Early in the morning on the first Sunday of December 2017, I
received an urgent text from my friend and pastor, Nirup Alphonse:
Hey T—Please pray. The team showed up to get the trailer and start set-
ting up church this morning, and it's gone. Meeting up with them now.

At the time, our church was mobile, a set-up-and-tear-down
gathering that uses space at the high school—and that trailer held everything from our screen and A/V system to our tithe baskets, Bibles, and
coffee maker and cups (you know, the important stuff). Over a hundred
thousand dollars' worth of what we would have said was important stuff
was in the trailer—and someone had taken all of it in the night.

Did we cancel church that morning? No way. We settled in tightly, squeezing close to one another as we worshiped and learned from Nirup's sermon. It was one of the most beautiful and meaningful services I've ever been part of. One of our local Denver news channels referred to the theft as a "Holy Heist"—and we kept not only the term but the lessons we learned from it.

Now on the first Sunday of December each year—the first Sunday of Advent—we also celebrate Holy Heist Sunday. We strip down to the basics. We don't use our lights and big sound system. We don't put up our screen and projector. We pass around Starbucks bags as we give our tithe. We go back to the essentials: community, the message of Jesus, and a whole lot of prayer.

Nirup often calls our community a House of Prayer, and we certainly were after the Holy Heist. Our relatively new little church plant didn't have a hundred thousand dollars in the bank to repurchase everything, but God generously answered our requests. First, a few larger local churches called, saying they had a check for us. And then smaller churches reached out with that same message. A body of believers out of state said they were sending money. Even a brand-new church that had only been open a Sunday or two generously gave to our little House of Prayer. We were astounded. And humbled. And thankful to be part of a community that also believes in the power of prayer.

A few days ago, we learned from Acts 16 that the church in Philippi was also a place of prayer. In fact, the church was literally born out of an outdoor House of Prayer by the river. And we discover in the letter to the Philippians that remembering and advocating for the believers in prayer was an integral part of Paul's relationship with this young church.

What if our lives were the same—built on a foundation of prayer? It might be easy to say we want that, but when we really stop to think about it, we might feel a bit daunted. Most of us believe in the power of prayer, yet we spend an incredibly small amount of time each day actually doing it. Not that we don't *want* to or that we don't think it's important. We just . . . don't do it much. (I certainly struggle with that!)

1. What does prayer look like in your life?

_____

_____

_____

_____

_____

_____

Here in Philippians 1:3, Paul says he thanks God every time he thinks about this group of believers. And he uses an interesting word for *thanks*: *eucharisteō* (εὐχαριστέω; pronounced *yoo-khar-is-teh-o*).

2. Does this word sound familiar to you at all? Why or why not?

_____

_____

The Eucharist is the celebration and remembrance of the Last Supper, which we observe today by taking Communion. We can find this word throughout the New Testament—and every time, it is used in conjunction with prayer (Acts 28:15; Romans 1:8; Ephesians 5:20). The Greek word *eucharisteō* literally means "to give thanks," "to be grateful, feel thankful."[17]

When one of our Ethiopian sons joined our family at the age of almost seven, he renamed himself Ezekiel. While we understood his decision—sometimes, adopted children choose a new name to express leaving one season of life and entering another—we were a bit wistful about the change. My husband and I adored the name his mama had given him: Temesgen (pronounced Tom-es-gen). In Ethiopia, *Temesgen* means the overwhelming, deep adoration and thankfulness you feel in your heart toward God. What a beautiful and significant name!

This is the kind of thankfulness I believe *eucharisteō* points us toward. Thankfulness with incredible depth and significance. One that consumes the innermost portions of our hearts and spills out into the world around us.

> Eucharisteo *means "to give thanks," and* give
> *is a verb, something that we do. God calls*
> *me* to do *thanks.* To give the thanks away.
> *That thanks-*giving *might literally become*
> thanks-*living. That our lives become the*
> *very blessings we have received.*
>
> *I am blessed. I can bless.* Imagine!
> *I could let Him make* me *the gift!*
>
> *I could* be *the joy!*[18]
>
> ANN VOSKAMP

3. How would you describe your feelings of thankfulness in your life and relationship with God? In what ways could you move more toward *Temesgen* and *eucharisteō* thankfulness?

Of course, maybe you feel like thankfulness just isn't compatible with the difficult season you're in. But remember—when Paul writes this letter to Philippi, he's in a Roman prison. He's awaiting trial, and he knows he may lose his life because of his love for Jesus. Even so—Paul praises God, joyfully thanking Him for his friends.

4. Consider a hard season you have walked through or are currently in. How have you fought for joy? Where has God met you with unexpected joy?

Paul's joy isn't just obligatory. In fact, these verses resound with exultation:

> Every time you cross my mind, I break out in exclamations
> of thanks to God. Each exclamation is a trigger to prayer.
> I find myself praying for you with a glad heart. I am so
> pleased that you have continued on in this with us, believing
> and proclaiming God's Message, from the day you heard it
> right up to the present. There has never been the slightest
> doubt in my mind that the God who started this great work
> in you would keep at it and bring it to a flourishing finish
> on the very day Christ Jesus appears.
> PHILIPPIANS 1:3-6, MSG

Wouldn't you love someone to give you a compliment like that? *I break out in exclamations of thanks to God. Each exclamation is a trigger to prayer.* Paul rejoices in the good work God has done in the lives of these people, and he quickly tells them that "there has never been the slightest doubt in my mind that the God who started this great work in you would keep at it and bring it to a flourishing finish."

Arriving at this flourishing finish isn't a passive thing. God is doing this great work in us, and He has promised to keep at it. But will we keep at it too? Will we learn to appreciate the work in progress, to listen to how He is calling us to grow, to pursue Him in the midst of the in-between? We are all becoming more like Him, and we have the privilege of joining Him in that work.

5. Flip over to Psalm 37:4 and write it down:

_____

_____

6. What do you think this verse means?

_____

_____

King David penned these words as part of a song in his later years, when he could look back and see the significance of the Lord's hand through every moment of his life. So we shouldn't read these words flippantly. God is not Santa Claus, who gives us things as long as we ask and we've been *good little girls*. This verse isn't saying that we can have anything we want as long as we ask.

But what David *is* saying is that when we delight ourselves in the Lord and spend time with Him through His Word and prayer, something begins to shift. The position of our heart starts to line up with God's. His desires become our desires. We long for the things He longs for.

As Paul prays for his friends—even while he sits in prison—he can hang on to joy because he delights in the Lord. He's doing the opposite of complaining in these verses because he's fully aligned with God's heart for the Philippians. Paul has seen the Creator of the universe do great and mighty things, and that reality brings him immense joy.

Paul shares in verse 7,

> It is right for me to feel this way about you all, because I
> hold you in my heart, for you are all partakers with me of
> grace, both in my imprisonment and in the defense and
> confirmation of the gospel.
>
> PHILIPPIANS 1:7

It doesn't matter if he's thrown in jail or standing on trial for spreading the gospel; Paul is unshaken, because he remembers the worth of all he does in the name of Jesus Christ. Nothing can alter what God has put into motion. Paul is reminding the Philippians of this, and when we read his words, we are also reminded that nothing—not our poor decisions, not our struggles, not our sin or the sin of others—can prevent God's plan from happening.

If he has said it will be so, it will be so.

If God has put something on your heart and you know without a shadow of a doubt that it is from Him, don't worry about the timing of it all. Press on. Continue praying and laying that foundation in your life. Grow in wisdom and knowledge by spending time in the Word. Be deeply rooted, and watch your heart align with His. He will bring His plans for you to fruition.

Meditate on 2 Thessalonians 1:11 and ask the Lord to calm your heart as you meet with Him in prayer. Remember—if He's prompted you to do something in faith, He will accomplish it.

All this is why we are constantly praying for you, so God will make you worthy of the great calling you have received from

Him and will give you the power to accomplish every good
intention and work of faith.

2 THESSALONIANS 1:11, VOICE

Amen.

WEEK 1 • *Day 5*

 READ PHILIPPIANS 1:9-11

When my kids were all still really little, I started writing their names
next to certain passages in my Bible, dedicating specific ones to each
child. I even printed out some of those verses and scrapbooked cute
little plaques for each child, posting them just outside the doors to
their rooms. I got the idea while reading this verse:

5 You shall love the LORD your God with all your heart and
with all your soul and with all your might. 6 And these words
that I command you today shall be on your heart. 7 You shall
teach them diligently to your children, and shall talk of them
when you sit in your house, and when you walk by the way,

and when you lie down, and when you rise. [8] You shall bind them as a sign on your hand, and they shall be as frontlets between your eyes. [9] You shall write them on the doorposts of your house and on your gates.

DEUTERONOMY 6:5-9

Growing roots is just the beginning of God's work in us. When our roots are established and we bear fruit, part of that fruit is bringing the love and truth of God into the lives of those around us. I put those verses on my kids' doors—and I teach in my church, and I write these studies—because I want to teach the hows and whys of loving God to those I do life with. I want to teach it to my children, to my neighbors, my friends, and anyone I encounter.

1. In what ways do you bring God's Word into your everyday relationships?

I smiled when I looked at our verses in my Bible today, because Ezekiel's name is next to Philippians 1:9-11. This passage is full of immense encouragement, but we're also going to dig into Paul's larger purpose in these words.

2. Write Philippians 1:9-11:

3. One of the beautiful ways God's Word can minister to us is by giving us language for our prayers. Have you ever prayed names into Scripture? Read verses 9 to 11 again, and ask God to bring someone to mind. Fill their name into the blanks:

> Lord Jesus, it is my prayer that _____'s love may abound more and more, with knowledge and all discernment, so that he/she may approve what is excellent, and so _____ may be pure and blameless for the day of Christ. Father, may _____ be filled with the fruit of righteousness that comes through Jesus Christ, to the glory and praise of God. Amen![19]

4. In addition to giving us language for prayer, God's Word can equip us to affirm and encourage others directly. Consider how someone might respond if you spoke those words over them:

> _____, I *know* that your love *will* abound more and more, with knowledge and all discernment, so that you, _____, *will* approve what is excellent, and so be pure and blameless for the day of Christ. _____, you *are* filled with the fruit of righteousness that comes through Jesus Christ, to the glory and praise of God!

Aren't these the kinds of words that speak life into another person? I learned the importance of life-giving words from my parents. When I was young and my brother Erik and I got caught being rude to each other, my folks would make us say five kind things about the other person as we apologized. I hated it. Erik hated it. But now as an adult I know the purpose of this exercise. If we want to build up those around us—and, in the case of my brother and me, if we want to move toward relational restoration—we must speak words that give life. (Of course, Erik and I would roll our eyes and say lame or backhanded compliments along the lines of "I like your hair" or "Your face looks less stupid when you smile," which of course thrilled our parents.)

Whenever I think of speaking life over someone, I immediately think of Donald Miller's book *Scary Close*. As Donald struggled through broken relationship after broken relationship, his friend Bob Goff chose to love him well through his words:

> "You don't sound fine," Bob said.
>
> I'd have argued with him, but I was afraid he'd notice I was slurring my words.
>
> "You know what I've noticed about you, Don?" Bob said.
>
> "What's that, Bob?"
>
> "I've noticed you're good at relationships."
>
> I said nothing. I wasn't sure I understood him correctly. Then he said it again, right into the silence of the phone.
>
> "You're good at relationships, Don," he repeated.
>
> The truth is I hadn't cried since I'd broken off the engagement. Like I said, I'd gone numb. But as he said those absurd words, something in me began to feel again and all the pain of the season swelled up. I pulled the phone from my ear, dropped my head on the desk, and wept. And as I cried, Bob kept repeating, "Don, you're good at relationships. You're still good at them. You've always been good at them."[20]

That's the kind of mom, wife, friend I'd like to be. In our divided culture, too often we find ourselves retreating to angry, defensive words—and we forget about the transformative power of loving, life-giving words.

5. In what practical ways can you speak life into someone today?

Now, I mentioned earlier that Paul was specific and intentional in his prayer for the Philippians. We're going to look a little closer at what Paul prays for to find out why his words are so life-giving.

"It is my prayer that your love may abound more and more." (Philippians 1:9)

The word that Paul uses here for *love* is *agapē* (ἀγάπη, pronounced *a-ga-pay*). The ancient Greek language has seven words for love, and *agapē* is the highest and most comprehensive form. *Agapē* is love without condition, built on selflessness, generosity, and compassion toward others. Jesus used the word *agapē* whenever He told us to love Him and love others. No fine print; no holds barred; no ifs, ands, or buts; no strings attached. This love is final and full and absolute. And that's what Paul is praying *may abound* in this verse.

6. Head on over to Philippians 1:9 in the BLB, tap on the verse, and select the phrase *may abound*. What does *perisseuō* (περισσεύω, pronounced *per-is-syoo-o*) mean?

That's a *lot* of love, right? Paul doesn't specify whom we should love this way, which can only mean one thing: We need to love everyone—whether or not we think they're worthy or we like them or we want to. You know why? Because Jesus loves them (John 13:34-35).

"With knowledge and all discernment" (verse 9)

Paul is also asking that the Philippians' love would abound "in knowledge and depth of insight" (NIV; "real knowledge and all discernment" in the NASB). (And don't forget—while Paul is writing this to the Philippians, these words are also for us!)

Picking up my phone again and heading to this passage in the BLB, I see that *real knowledge* or *epignōsis* (ἐπίγνωσις, pronounced *ep-i-gno-sis*) means "precise and correct knowledge . . . of things ethical and divine."[21] Correct knowledge means to be in possession of precise and exact understanding of something. But how is this different from *discernment*?

7. Go to the *Interlinear* for Philippians 1:9 on the BLB, and look up *aisthēsis* (αἴσθησις, pronounced *ais-thay-sis*). How would you differentiate this from correct knowledge?

Discernment has to do with perception—understanding connected to our hearts and the Holy Spirit's guidance. Knowledge has to do with information, understanding in relation to our brains. Discernment and knowledge are both important. Love doesn't mean ignoring poor behavior, character, or choices; knowledge informs our understanding of right and wrong, wise and unwise. But even as we understand those things, discernment helps us to know how to respond—how to speak life and not judgment into other people. Discernment also leads us to guide, protect, and place boundaries.

Being discerning means being perceptive as you pore over what you know and apply knowledge in a practical way.

8. How can you be discerning without being judgmental?

In John 7:24, Jesus says to the crowd listening to Him, "Don't be hypercritical; use your head—and heart!—to discern what is right, to test what is authentically right" (MSG). He is the perfect example of recognizing behavior as wrong and hating evil yet still showing compassion. It's the very definition of discernment, right? Judging carries with it condemnation and a condescending attitude. We're not to place someone beneath us; we're to love them right where we both are, realizing that we all struggle.

"So that you may approve what is excellent" (verse 10)

The term *may approve* is translated as *dokimazō* (δοκιμάζω, pronounced *do-ki-mahd-zo*) which, as we learn from the BLB, essentially means "to test, examine, prove, scrutinise (to see whether a thing is genuine or not)."[22] This term was particularly used when testing the authenticity of coins,[23] which feels like such a solid, visible example of the importance of authenticity. None of us want to have a pocket of fraudulent coinage . . . and none of us want a heart full of fraudulence and inauthenticity. By being able to discern what is best and substantial, we're able to recognize what really matters in life.

I love the way *The Message* translates this passage:

This is my prayer: that your love will flourish and that you will not only love much but well. Learn to love appropriately. You need to use your head and test your feelings so that your love is sincere and intelligent, not

sentimental gush. Live a lover's life, circumspect and
exemplary, a life Jesus will be proud of.

I always want exact instructions in life. Like: If I do this, then
that will happen. You know, *A + B = C*. I love that Paul gives us
this type of instruction (we'll talk more about this in week 6). To
live an authentic life, we need to "learn to love appropriately," to
"use [our] head and test [our] feelings so that [our] love is sincere
and intelligent." We need to "live a lover's life . . . a life Jesus will
be proud of."

So let's be lovers of people. Not in a romantic way (though that's
good too) but by striving to be the kind of woman who loves everybody. All the time. No matter what. That's a radical concept, isn't it?
I know, I get it. I can think of people who are very different from me,
who drive me nuts, who are even toxic or dangerous, and sometimes
I think I don't want to—or even shouldn't—love them. The thing is:
It doesn't say we need to be best friends with them or that we need
to approve of their behavior. But we do need to love them as God
loves them, because as much as we'd like to turn our backs from the
fact sometimes, they are His children too. He loves those hard-to-like
people every bit as much as He loves us.

"And so be pure and blameless for the day of Christ" (verse 10)

If we love the way Paul is encouraging us to here, we'll be able to discern how to live a life that is pure (translated in the BLB as *sincere*[24])
and blameless. As Bible commentator Frank Thielman puts it, "Paul's
basic request for the Philippians . . . is that they might express their
love in ways that show both a knowledge of how to obey God's will
generally, and, more specifically, of how to make moral decisions
based on God's will in the give-and-take of everyday living."[25] Ben
and I are always telling our kids that "words matter," and I think
that's partially what Paul is trying to say here. Words overflow from

the health of our heart, so if we're speaking death (unkindness or gossip), it's likely our heart isn't in a good place. But if we are women who speak life (kindness and encouragement) into others, we not only will be sincere—not causing others to stumble—but will over-flow with what Paul talks about next in this passage.

"Filled with the fruit of righteousness that comes through Jesus Christ, to the glory and praise of God" (verse 11)

We learn in Galatians 5:22-23 that the fruit given to us by the Spirit results in love, joy, peace, patience, goodness, faithfulness, gentleness, and self-control. In this passage from Philippians, we're learning what ethical fruit we will bear when we live intentionally and with love. Paul doesn't want us focused on an exterior life of striving and attempting to look good through what we do. No—he's encouraging us to live a fruit-filled life, where God's restoration of our hearts and souls emerges outward into action. If we plant this seed of love into our hearts, the outward fruit will be good works, living the way God calls us to—but because that seed grows from Living Water, it is authentic and sustain-able in a way willing ourselves to live rightly never could be. In other words, the fruit described here is rooted from the heart.

As much as we all want to be people who speak life-giving words over others, none of us do it perfectly—or perfectly consistently. We get frustrated by that one passive-aggressive coworker and make snide remarks behind their back. We snap at our children when they move out the door at a snail's pace. We nitpick at our spouses when they don't do things quite the way we wish they would. We get frustrated with our parents, neglect our friends, are impatient with the cashier at the grocery store.

But as we pursue the life that really matters, as we seek for our love to abound more and more, we'll find ourselves being more inten-tional with our words. We'll find ourselves slower to speak when we're grumpy. We'll see the needs around us more clearly and sense God's prompting about the right words to speak.

Let's commit to being women who speak life. And as we do . . .
I think we'll start to see life spring up in new ways in the people
around us.

Come to Jesus with a humble heart, asking for His forgive-
ness for the times you've failed to speak life. He is full of grace,
and He knows we simply can't do life well without Him. Ask
Him who you need to chat with to apologize for your words—
or who you need to reach out to with words of hope and
affirmation.

Amen.

WEEK 1 • *Notes*

Share your biggest takeaways from this week:

Choosing Joy

Philippians 1:12-26

WEEK 2 ● *Day 1*

 READ PHILIPPIANS 1:12-14

Want to know how mature you are in your faith? See what it takes to rob you of your joy.

Paul's letter to the Philippians is famous for its statements about joy, but his words should really make us consider the depth of faith those statements emerged from. Paul was imprisoned in Rome two times, and he was martyred at the end of the second time. This first time, he was under house arrest. And this house arrest wasn't like Martha Stewart being confined to her sprawling multimillion-dollar estate for five months. Paul was chained to a guard twenty-four hours a day for two years. In case you're wondering, that's 17,520 hours of never having a single second of time alone. (For an introvert like me, that sounds like a whole 'nother level of torture.) To survive during this time, he depended entirely on gifts (monetary and otherwise).

 History Lesson

Even though house arrest was tough, it was still far better than being thrown in prison during this time period. Why did Paul receive the relative privilege of house arrest? There were several reasons:

1. He was a Roman citizen (see Acts 16:37-40 for some context).[1]

2. He had not committed a heinous crime and was not considered politically dangerous.

3. He had already received favorable verdicts from governors Festus and Agrippa.

4. The Praetorian guard oversaw his imprisonment. (More on them later.)

Paul's chained-to-the-guard experience reminds me of something my husband, Ben, told me about. Ben had, shall we say, a colorful and difficult childhood. While at a boarding school for troubled kids, he'd sometimes get himself into further trouble, which resulted in something called Hip Restriction. Hip Restriction meant that the boy being disciplined had to stay within six feet of the dean. When the dean went to the restroom, the boy had to stand outside. When the dean had a meeting, the boy had to sit by the door. Wherever the dean walked, the boy trailed behind him. This could go on for days, depending on the severity of what the boy had done. Ben says it was *awful*, and I can guarantee he griped and complained his way through every Hip Restriction. And we'd expect to see something similar from Paul, right? His house arrest was way longer than just a few days, and that chain was probably only about eighteen inches long.[2]

1. What sense of Paul's attitude do you get from Philippians 1:12-14?

Paul isn't angry or discouraged or depressed. No—instead, he's basically saying, "*I am in chains, but the gospel is not!*"

 ### *History Lesson*

FIRST MISSIONARY JOURNEY (ACTS 13:4–14:25)[3]

On his first journey, Paul set out from Antioch, which was the third-largest city in the world (behind Rome and Alexandria). As he began, Paul and his companions traveled to the southern cities of Galatia. From there he went to Perga, Antioch in Pisidia (different from the city of Antioch), and a handful of other cities, before returning to Antioch.

SECOND MISSIONARY JOURNEY (ACTS 15:35–18:22)[4]

The second missionary journey took Paul again across Asia Minor, traveling to Derbe, Lystra, Phrygia, and then Troas. It's during this trip that God altered Paul's plans and led him over to Europe for the first time—into Philippi, Berea (see Acts 17:10-12), and Athens. Athens, as you may know, was the cultural center of all Greek culture and was known for its renowned philosophers: Socrates, Plato, and Aristotle. In fact, the philosophical point of view of those in Athens shaped the mindset of the entire Roman Empire.

From Athens, Paul traveled over to the wealthy seaport city of Corinth (and established the church, eventually writing several letters to the Corinthian believers). As a port city, Corinth was a busy hub and home to an outdoor theatre (seating over twenty thousand people) for athletic games (second only to the Olympic Games). Corinth was considered the commercial center of the ancient world. From there, Paul journeyed back to Asia Minor, traveling to the commercial, political, and religious city of Ephesus, where he established the Ephesian church.

THIRD MISSIONARY JOURNEY (ACTS 18:23–21:22)[5]

Paul's third and last missionary journey strategically reached the biggest and most populated centers of the ancient world, and the hope of the gospel began to spread like wildfire across the globe. This journey followed a path similar to that of his second trip. As Paul shared the message of Jesus in Jerusalem, he was arrested, and eventually the authorities decided to send him to Rome. On their way to the capital city, Paul and many other prisoners were shipwrecked (see the incredible story in Acts 27–28). After he finally made it to Rome, Paul was put under house arrest for two years, during which time he wrote many letters, including those to the Ephesians, Philippians, Colossians, and Philemon.

Paul had wanted to go to Rome for years, but God's plan for his time there looked far different from how he likely anticipated. Instead of preaching the Word of God in the marketplace or public forums, Paul instead preached to his guards and anyone who came to see him.

In Philippians 1:12, Paul proclaims that everything that has happened to him "has really served to advance the gospel." He certainly doesn't sound like a guy who feels defeated after losing his freedom. But how on earth has his imprisonment *advanced* the Kingdom of God?

2. Please pen down what Paul says in verse 13:

 History Lesson

The Praetorian Guard were a different level of Roman soldier. These men were the elite of the elite (think Special Forces, the FBI, and the Secret Service group combined), handpicked because of their superior abilities and given a double portion of salary. They worked as personal bodyguards for Caesar. They worked as firefighters; managed crowd control at athletic events; and even had their hand in the secret police, coups, and controlling Caesar himself.[6]

3. Why did the Praetorian Guard's role in guarding Paul benefit the gospel?

_____

_____

_____

If Paul had been able to share the news of Jesus freely around Rome, he would have reached many of the normal, everyday people of the city, to be sure. But in prison, he had the ear of the most specialized and hard-core group of soldiers in the entire Roman Empire—Paul spent 17,520 hours of one-on-one time with those who worked in Caesar's household and reported to Caesar himself. Over his two-year sentence, he likely had as many as two dozen guards[7] . . . which means at least twenty-four high-ranking officers who could spread his message to countless others in high-ranking positions.

Even if these guards didn't ultimately believe in the Good News of Jesus, any publicity is good publicity, right? After being chained to Paul for hours, these men would have heard every part of his story, every part of God's work, every part of what these Jesus followers believed. Even speaking negatively about the gospel would have spread the gospel. God can use any interaction to His benefit and open even the hardest of hearts.

In verse 14, we read that Paul's bravery in sharing the message of Jesus during his imprisonment encouraged the entire body of believers. God can do incredible things when even one person lets their love for Jesus overcome their fears.

4. What struggles in your life have amplified God's Good News to those around you?

_____

_____

_____

God doesn't give the hardest battles to His toughest soldiers;
He creates the toughest soldiers through life's hardest battles.

UNKNOWN

5. Did your faith mature in your struggle? If so, how? If that season shook your faith, can you look back and see any beauty God may have drawn from those ashes?

When you replace *Why is this happening to me?* with *What is this trying to teach me?*, everything shifts.

Several years ago, one of our kids told our social worker that I was abusing them. They'd only been home from Ethiopia for a short time and were struggling in so many ways, coming to terms with the fact that real life in the US was different from what they saw in the movies. Learning English is difficult, and so is living with a family when you've never really had one before. Even harder? Learning love for the first time in your life when your past is filled with trauma.

Child Protective Services (CPS) began a full-blown investigation. They talked to my family, to my friends. They met with my children and my husband and threatened to take not only this hurting child but *all* my children away. Our world was on the brink of falling apart simply because our child thought the lie would make us put them back on a plane to Ethiopia. It was terrifying and devastating.

But every time I prayed during those weeks of unknown outcome, the Lord whispered these words into my heart: *I am allowing you to go through this for a reason.*

I have a tattoo on my wrist with the words *send me*. It's the reminder of my decades-old prayer of submission to Christ. Long before this child had even been born, I whispered the words, "Use me, send me." Use me for what? I didn't know. Send me where? I had no clue.

Now, I saw where I would be used and sent. Where I could make a difference for the Kingdom. In the life of a wounded child. Before a world watching how I would respond to betrayal.

Our child saw that we didn't give up on them. And they saw that even in the midst of the worst thing they could think to do to us, we still loved them deeply and unconditionally. (Thankfully CPS saw this too.) We forgave. We rooted ourselves deeper in God and with each other.

Suffering seasons show who we really are in Christ, to everyone around us—and who Jesus is in us. Paul showed the Praetorian Guard who Jesus was in the middle of imprisonment. I showed my child who He was in the face of having my family torn apart. We both got the opportunity to show a watching world how good, gracious, and loving He is.

> Love never gives up.
> Love cares more for others than for self.
> Love doesn't want what it doesn't have.
> Love doesn't strut,
> Doesn't have a swelled head,
> Doesn't force itself on others,
> Isn't always "me first,"
> Doesn't fly off the handle,
> Doesn't keep score of the sins of others,

Doesn't revel when others grovel,
Takes pleasure in the flowering of truth,
Puts up with anything,
Trusts God always,
Always looks for the best,
Never looks back,
But keeps going to the end.

1 CORINTHIANS 13:4-7, MSG

If God is love (1 John 4:8), then He is all of these things. They literally embody who He is. His love for us in the midst of our struggle upholds us and equips us to live in joy.

If you're particularly struggling in the current season you're in, rest in God's love for you. Put God's name in the blank as a reminder of who He is and how with Him, you can be and do all these things. Then, in the space at the end of today, ask Him to restore your joy as you sink deeply into the truth of His love for you.

_____ never gives up

_____ cares more for others than for self

_____ doesn't want what He doesn't have

_____ doesn't strut

_____ doesn't have a swelled head

_____ doesn't force Himself on others

_____ isn't always "me first"

_____ doesn't fly off the handle

_____ doesn't keep score of the sins of others

_____ doesn't revel when others grovel

_____ takes pleasure in the flowering of truth

_____ puts up with anything

_____ trusts God always

_____ always looks for the best

_____ never looks back

_____ never gives up, but keeps going to the end[8]

_____

_____

_____

_____

_____

_____

_____

_____

_____

_____

_____

_____

Amen.

WEEK 2 • *Day 2*

 READ PHILIPPIANS 1:15-18

Have you ever struggled with someone else because they have what you want?

Her business is more successful than yours. She's married, and you haven't had a date since *The Office* first aired. She has kids, and you've been struggling with infertility for years. She just finished a gorgeous whole-home remodel, while you're just praying the hinges of your kitchen cabinets hold on a little bit longer. You want to write a book, and she just signed a contract for five. You're covered in baby spit up and haven't showered in . . . *um* . . . *two* . . . *no,* three*! Has it really been* three *days?!* and she drops her kids off at preschool in stilettos, with perfectly blown-out hair.

Sigh. Grimace.

I get it. I've felt most of these things myself. And social media can amplify these feelings, right? I've made myself unfollow some women I truly love and admire because admiration has crept into envy.

Envy has a lot of dark sides. Unhealthy ambition, which envy is a symptom of, causes us to push other people down. Maybe we're tinged with happiness when that woman we envy struggles in some way—she got a really bad haircut, or her perfect-looking marriage is in shambles, or her Harvard-bound son got in some legal trouble. We can start to see another person's struggle as our benefit.

All that feels yucky, doesn't it?

Well, that's basically what Paul is talking about in Philippians today.

He doesn't share all the details, but he knows that some folks are preaching the gospel out of selfish ambition. They're likely thrilled that he has been arrested and see his absence as an opportunity.

1. What is the focus of these people's ambition?

Christ? Furthering the gospel? Empowering the body of believers? Nope. Self.

Yeesh.

We find this phrase *selfish ambition* (*eritheia;* ἐριθεία, pronounced *e-ri-thay-ah*) in several places within the Bible, including James and Philippians.

2. What are the main points of the following verses? (If you have time, read the passages in several translations—even head to the BLB and dig into the Greek!)

James 3:14-18

_____

_____

_____

_____

Philippians 2:2-4

_____

_____

_____

_____

If we look up *eritheia* (ἐριθεία) on Bible Hub, we find that it literally means "acting for one's own gain."[9] Have you ever been on the receiving end of this kind of treatment? Maybe someone has kicked you when you were down, swooped in and tried to benefit from your misfortune. If you've found yourself there, you have an idea how Paul might have felt when he wrote these verses.

3. When someone else treats you poorly or takes advantage of your hard situation, how do you respond? What does Paul's response teach us about how to remain healthy and Christ-focused in the face of this kind of treatment?

_____

_____

_____

_____

You may encounter many defeats,
but you must not be defeated.[10]

MAYA ANGELOU

Paul doesn't defend himself or try to bolster his stature. He doesn't bad-mouth the people who are relishing his imprisonment. Instead, he refocuses the conversation on what really matters: God can use even selfish ambition for His ultimate gain.

Because Paul's focus is on Christ and not on himself, he doesn't really care what these other guys are saying behind his back. Even if these prideful individuals are preaching out of envy and rivalry rather than the genuine desire to share the gospel—people are still hearing God's message! Paul says in Philippians 1:18,

How am I to respond? I've decided that I really don't care about their motives, whether mixed, bad, or indifferent. Every time one of them opens his mouth, Christ is proclaimed, so I just cheer them on!

MSG

God can use anything for His glory. But He'd much rather use our redeemed hearts and our love for one another (John 13:35). How can we be women who build one another up instead of tearing each other down or being silently gleeful at another's misfortune? There is enough room at the table for all of us, and we are stronger together. When did we start believing the lie that we can't all win? That God can't use all of us, amid both our similarities and our differences?

4. Do you struggle to genuinely and authentically root for someone in your life? What envy or resentment does God need to uproot in your heart?

5. What are some practical ways you can lift up the women around you this week?

_____

_____

_____

Let's be women who truly see and celebrate the significance of others. Let's lift up those around us, encouraging them and affirming their gifts and value. When we choose authenticity and partnership instead of selfishness and envy, we will be living in pursuit of what ultimately matters: the Good News of Jesus infusing and affecting everyone around us.

Spend some time talking to the Lord about someone in your life who is difficult to love. Ask Him to uproot any bitterness or envy and help you to instead pray for their wholeness and flourishing.

_____

_____

_____

_____

_____

_____

_____

_____

_____

_____

_____

Amen.

WEEK 2 • *Day 3*

 READ PHILIPPIANS 1:19-21

Fear of death is not an unusual thing. I think most of us have some trepidation about the whole dying thing—what it will feel like, when it will happen, how it will affect the people around us.

But the thing is . . . I'm actually not afraid to die. I'm crazy excited to go to heaven. I'm not saying I especially want to go tomorrow or anything—I'm just enthusiastic about the moment I eventually arrive. I know it's beyond anything we can wrap our minds around, but I've imagined what it will be like quite a bit. I'll worship God with my new set of Whitney Houston-esque pipes (God and I have already discussed this at length). I won't get migraines or experience heartache. I'll sit on a front porch and have a cool glass of strawberry lemonade with Farmor (my Swedish grandmother) and our chocolate lab, Thatcher. I'll get to see colors I can't even begin to describe here on earth. I'm excited about being with the diverse people of God without the judgment that so often divides and wounds us. And I'm eager to ask lots and lots of questions—to sit at the feet of Jesus, and to ask Eve what the Garden was like, and to learn from Jonathan about how he remained such a good friend to David through such turmoil and family strife.

When we follow Jesus, we get the extraordinary opportunity to live life not just without fear of death, but with anticipation for what's beyond. That should change how we live—how we think about our actions here and now, how we relate to the people around us. We can set aside our worries about what might happen because we already know what *will* happen. And that's what we see from Paul in our verses today: a rightsized understanding of life and how we're to live in light of what God has done.

We're going to spend a bit of time in the BLB today, so let's hop into Philippians 1:19 and go straight to the *Interlinear*.

1. Tap on the phrase *will turn out* (*apobainō*; ἀποβαίνω, pronounced *a-po-bai-no*). What strikes you as unexpected about this particular term?

_____

_____

_____

_____

I find it interesting that Paul used a verb associated with boating. (That certainly doesn't emerge from our English reading of the text, does it?) Paul likely wanted to create a mental picture for those reading his letter—a visual of their prayers cutting loose the mooring, weighing anchor, and then setting sail.

We often forget the impact prayer has on our lives and the lives of those we bring before God, and here Paul is reminding the Philippians (and us) that the result of prayer is action and movement. For Paul, prayer moves him into a perspective that his suffering will glorify Jesus Christ, one way or another. Perhaps he feels as though he's disembarking from fear and stepping onto the solid ground of the path God has called him to walk.

2. In your everyday life, how can you choose to turn from safety and walk into a life of boldness?

_____

_____

_____

_____

_____

In these verses, Paul isn't resigned to his fate. He's leaning into what's ahead, boldly moving forward. If we read his words in *The Message*, we can better understand his overall tone and feeling:

> I'm going to keep that celebration going because I know how it's going to turn out. Through your faithful prayers and the generous response of the Spirit of Jesus Christ, everything he wants to do in and through me will be done. I can hardly wait to continue on my course. I don't expect to be embarrassed in the least. On the contrary, everything happening to me in this jail only serves to make Christ more accurately known, regardless of whether I live or die. They didn't shut me up; they gave me a platform! Alive, I'm Christ's messenger; dead, I'm his bounty. Life versus even more life! I can't lose.
>
> PHILIPPIANS 1:19-21, MSG

3. Using this version of the passage, fill in the following blanks:

I'm going to keep that celebration going because _____

_____ .

I can hardly wait_____ .

I don't expect _____ .

On the contrary,_____

_____

_____ .

Paul's last line in verse 21 kind of reminds me of that famous line from *Friday Night Lights*: "Clear eyes, full hearts, can't lose."[11] Paul has clear eyes. He understands the magnitude of what he's doing. His heart is not only full but overflowing with love for Christ. And because he loves God so much, no matter what the outcome, he simply cannot lose. He's not looking at life versus death. He's anticipating life versus everlasting life with God.

4. How do you feel about the idea of dying? What frightens you?
What encourages you?

5. What is your reaction to Paul's perspective on death in these
verses?

When we understand what death means for Jesus followers, we
can truly grasp the gravity and opportunity of life right now. As
writer and speaker Eddie Kaufholz once wrote,

> We are put on this earth for a reason. If there was no reason,
> God wouldn't have put us here. He doesn't need us to
> hang out in this holding pen for 80+ years, there's room in
> heaven. But God chose to put us here—and to live. Live
> abundantly, live gratefully, live justly, and live to accomplish
> the work of God. Am I afraid of the afterlife? No. But am
> I just human enough to not be able to fully comprehend
> heaven and, therefore, be afraid of saying goodbye to my
> sweet wife, daughters, friends, homebrewing, crisp fall air,
> laughing so hard I cry, happy little existence that I've eked
> out? Yes. Because this is the heaven I know—and I like
> getting to live in God's creation.
>   . . . There's no need to be afraid of death. But, there's no
> reason why you wouldn't be. My encouragement to you is
> to do all you can to figure out why God has put you on this
> globe, and leave your tomorrows to Him.[12]

You are immortal until God's work for you
is done. You really will not die. You will
not die until God intends for you to die.
This is wonderful. I mean, where else
would you rather rest than in this?[13]

JOHN PIPER

Paul knew that God had placed him on earth for a reason, and he was ready to be with God whenever that work was done. God's work in us and through us infuses our time here with meaning, and His promise of life with Him means that our death also has meaning and hope. We're not optimists if we believe this: We are realists. This is the reality of our life with God. And that is what Paul celebrates in Philippians 1:21.

6. Philippians 1:21 is one of the most well-known verses in the entire New Testament. Write it here:

_____

_____

_____

_____

_____

7. Let's head back over to the BLB and dig into the original Greek of this verse. How does the *Interlinear* help us understand the full meaning of the word *live* (*zaō*; ζάω, pronounced *zah-oh*)?

_____

_____

_____

_____

I love the meaning "to be in full vigour,"[14] don't you? It's such an exceptional visual: to truly savor and relish life, to breathe and flourish. To live isn't to simply drift along and exist. Paul is talking about living vibrantly and fully.

Let's tap on verse 21 in the BLB again and click on *Text Commentaries*. Feel free to check any of the commentary writers who have something to share on Philippians 1, but we're going to look a little more closely at what Matthew Henry has to say (click on his "Commentary on Philippians 1," and scroll down to where it says "Phl 1:21-26").

8. After reading this little section, write down your biggest takeaways.

_____

_____

_____

_____

_____

_____

_____

_____

_____

_____

_____

_____

9. How would you reword Henry's observations here?

_____

_____

_____

The enemy doesn't realize that sending so many troubles our way can drive us into the arms of the Lord. When we find ourselves in pain and struggle, God is our source of restoration and hope. Sometimes that restoration is here and now: As in the life of Paul, our struggle can become a platform for God's Good News in the lives of others, or a means for making us more like Him. As Lysa TerKeurst reminds us in her book *It's Not Supposed to Be This Way*:

> God doesn't want you or me to suffer. But He will allow it in doses to increase our trust. Our pain and suffering isn't to hurt us. It's to save us. To save us from a life where we are self-reliant, self-satisfied, self-absorbed, and set up for the greatest pain of all . . . separation from God.[15]

Even if God does not give us a glimpse of restoration in this life, the restoration in our far-better-life-to-come is a certainty. Wholeness and healing await us in life eternal with God. In this life we will have trouble (John 16:33), but trouble does not get the final word.

Talk to God about what His purposes might be in any hard situations or seasons you're walking through. Ask Him to allow what you're going through to bring a different kind of depth to your joy.

Amen.

WEEK 2 • *Day 4*

 READ PHILIPPIANS 1:22-24

Do you ever feel like you have too many decisions to make in a day? I sure do. Some of them are little decisions, like what to make for breakfast or whether to wear heels or flats. Other decisions are bigger and more difficult, like finding a more intensive therapist for a couple of our kids.

If you include my husband and me, I'm in charge of eight people (he totally counts himself as my seventh kid), and all the decision-making for this many people can be intimidating and exhausting. No matter if you're making decisions for a whole family or carrying your world on your own shoulders, it's probably the same for you: Life can sometimes be daunting with so many choices.

One of our kids often writes up a pros-and-cons list when he's about to step forward (or not) into something big. Today's passage in Philippians feels a bit like that as Paul goes back and forth between two pretty big possibilities: stay alive, or be with his Lord in heaven.

I visualize these verses a bit like a play or movie—Paul walking back and forth (dragging an exhausted guard by his side), wearing a rut in the ground beneath his feet, talking out loud about death versus life. But because Paul is an optimist, this is no pros-and-cons list—he goes right for the pros.

1. Read through this passage and write out Paul's pros-and-pros list:

PRO (LIVE)	PRO (DIE)

The Pro (Die) section isn't all that long, is it? It's hard to top the pro of being with Christ. Paul is exhausted. He's likely tired of living without his freedom. He's been chased by angry mobs, he's been left for dead after being stoned, he's been lost at sea. What could be better than going to heaven, where there is no more pain, fear, and exhaustion?

When Farmor (my Swedish grandmother) was on her deathbed, my family and I spent a lot of time at her bedside. Each day, we watched her draw closer to her new home, and she started telling us what she was seeing. Her eyes darted around the room as she saw things we definitely could not. With a slight smile, she told us that she could see a group of people gathering at the Gate, preparing a party for her, welcoming her home.

At one point, I was alone with my sweet grandmother and cuddled next her, recounting our many years of fun memories together. Suddenly she stopped me, with more gumption than I'd seen in days: "Chains! I hear chains! There aren't supposed to be *chains* in heaven!"

As I lifted my arm to brush hair out of her eyes, she again uttered an upset, "Chains!"—and I realized that my wrist-full of bracelets sounded very much like the chains that were agitating her. Once I showed her how my bracelets clinked against one another, she relaxed again. "I knew there were no chains," she whispered quietly.

Paul knew there were no chains in heaven. And after two years of sores and callouses from the thick and heavy metal, he likely found the idea of no chains immensely appealing. But . . . this is where the Pro (Live) column comes in: Paul sees how much he's still needed. And somehow, the idea of laboring for the good of the church gives him the desire to keep living, to not give up or give in.

Paul says in verse 22, "If I am to live in the flesh, that means fruitful labor for me."

2. What do you think Paul meant by "fruitful labor"?

_____

_____

_____

_____

_____

_____

_____

_____

"Better to lose your life than to waste it."[16] In John Piper's book *Why I Love the Apostle Paul: 30 Reasons*, I have this quote underlined with a heart and arrow in the margin. I don't want to waste my life. If I waste my one and only life, what was the point of *me*? If I live an ordinary life full of comfort and am not willing to run after what God has called me to, why keep me here?

3. Head on over to thesaurus.com and type in the word *fruitful*. Write down the words that jump out at you:

_____

_____

_____

_____

4. Do these words describe you and your life? Why or why not?

_____

_____

_____

When I looked up the word *fruitful* (*karpos*; καρπός, pronounced *kar-pos*) in the *Interlinear* section of the BLB, I scrolled down to see where else in the Bible that word has been used. One place it's used (over and over) is Matthew 7.

5. Circle all the times *fruit* is used in these verses:

¹⁶ But you will recognize them by their fruits. You don't find sweet, delicious grapes growing on thorny bushes, do you? You don't find delectable figs growing in the midst of prickly thistles. ¹⁷ People and their lives are like trees. Good trees bear beautiful, tasty fruit, but bad trees bear ugly, bitter fruit. ¹⁸ A good tree cannot bear ugly, bitter fruit; nor can a bad tree bear fruit that is beautiful and tasty. ¹⁹ And what happens to the rotten trees? They are cut down. They are used for firewood. ²⁰ When a prophet comes to you and preaches this or that, look for his fruits: sweet or sour? rotten or ripe?

MATTHEW 7:16-20, VOICE

6. Although this passage refers to false prophets (teachers or leaders who are deceiving those they influence), we can consider how the principles apply to any of us. How do these verses say we will recognize authentic believers?

_____

_____

_____

7. Write verse 17 in your own words:

_____

_____

_____

8. We know Paul is a trustworthy leader. He's truly the real deal, right? In what ways could his life continue to bear fruit, even as he was in prison?

_____

_____

_____

Paul says in Philippians 1:24 that "to remain in the flesh is more necessary on your account." In other words, Paul recognizes that continuing in a life full of ups and downs, weakness and struggle would benefit the Philippian church and the entire body of believers far more than his death ever could. Being a voice for God's Good News, taking it to the ends of the earth, speaking truth to the powers of the day, encouraging the people of God to live out their faith—all of those things were worth living for. Deep down, Paul knows that his life on earth needs to continue, that he must persist in fruitfulness so others may grow in the love of Christ and that Christ may be glorified through all he does. No giving up now.

Our sweet youngest daughter Elsabet learned the word _fruitful_ in preschool and has been using it slightly incorrectly ever since. She's always saying stuff like, "Mommy, today was fruitful" or "I'm feeling fruitful," meaning she had a good day at school, is feeling joyful, or made some right decisions. But even though that's not how we might typically use the word *fruitful*, doesn't Elsabet's understanding reflect what Paul is talking about here? May our labor be full of goodness, joy, and right decisions as we love God and love others well.

Talk to God about where you're anchoring your roots and spreading your limbs, readying yourself to bloom and produce fruit—and ask Him to reveal what might be hindering your fruitfulness.

Amen.

WEEK 2 • *Day 5*

   READ PHILIPPIANS 1:24-26

A few days ago, things at home were rough. And when I say rough, I mean *rough*. Several of the kids fought all day, derailing our plans; some unexpected financial needs arose; Ben was out of town; and hardest of all, we were entering something really huge and messy and uncertain with one of the kids.

When I walked into the girls' room to tuck them into bed, I discovered that the space we had cleaned together earlier in the day was now ravaged by a kid-induced tornado. I started bawling. Emotionally, I was spent. As my shoulders heaved with deep sobs, my teenager Ezekiel came in to check on me. He gave me a bear hug, and we sat together on the cluttered rug by the girls' bunk bed as he asked what had happened and I stained the shoulder of his T-shirt with mascara.

"It's too much, buddy," I said. "This is all just too much. I don't know how to do it. I don't know how to get through it."

Sometimes, even when we're walking in alignment with God, life still feels out of whack . . . because life is hard. Sometimes it's harder than hard. And during these moments, we have to be reminded to rest in the knowledge that *I cannot do it, but He can.*[17]

WHEN I SAY . . .	GOD SAYS . . .
"I'm too tired."	"I will give you rest." (Matthew 11:28)
"I can't go on."	"My grace is sufficient." (2 Corinthians 12:9)
"It's impossible."	"All things are possible." (Matthew 19:26)

WHEN I SAY . . .	GOD SAYS . . .
"I don't know how."	"I will direct your steps." (Proverbs 16:9, my paraphrase)
"I'm not able to."	"I am able to." (Ephesians 3:20, my paraphrase)
"I'm not worth it."	"You are worthwhile and important." (Matthew 10:29-31, my paraphrase)
"I'm afraid."	"Cast all your cares on Me." (1 Peter 5:7, my paraphrase)
"I can't do it."	"I will supply all your needs." (Philippians 4:19, my paraphrase)

Sometimes life really is too much. I cannot do things myself. But with Christ by my side, holding my hand and leading me step-by-step, I can do anything. So can Paul. And so can you.

> *I believe that suffering is part of the narrative, and that nothing really good gets built when everything's easy. I believe that loss and emptiness and confusion often give way to new fullness and wisdom.*[18]
> SHAUNA NIEQUIST

1. Let's dig into how God equips us to carry on when life gets too hard. What verb do we see in both Philippians 1:24 and 1:25?

Would you be surprised to discover that these two *remain* words are different? In verse 24, the word *remain* is *epimenō* (ἐπιμένω, pronounced *e-pee-men-o*) and means "to persevere," "the blessing for which one keeps himself fit," "to abide, to continue."[19]

2. Head back to the BLB, click on verse 25, and navigate to the *Interlinear*. What does *remain* or *menō* (μένω, pronounced *men-o*) mean?

Why do these two words have essentially the same meaning? Well, look at the first Greek word, *epimenō*, again. See any overlap? That's right: It contains within it the word *menō*, which is our second word for *remain*. Are your eyes glazing over? Stay with me; I really do have an important point. The word *epi* or ἐπί (pronounced *e-pee*) is a preposition. When *epi* connects with *menō*, it denotes motion alongside rest. Read that again: motion alongside rest. In other words, movement and rest harmonize and become one. When we're holding tightly to rest while moving forward, this is when we find perseverance!

3. How does rest equip us for movement and perseverance?

After digging into the Greek, I decided to reword these verses as a declaration for my own life:

I want to remain (*epimenō*) in the flesh because I can take rest in full dependence on Christ while tenaciously continuing, making a difference for the gospel. Convinced of this, I know I will remain (*menō*)—that with Him at the helm, I will endure and persevere, abiding with my community as we grow in joy in the faith.

4. Your turn! Rephrase Philippians 1:24-25 to reflect your own hope in Christ:

_____

_____

_____

_____

_____

In verse 25, Paul suddenly decides: He is "convinced of this" (meaning that he is to remain in the flesh) and plans to continue with "you all." He goes from wavering back and forth to proclaiming he will, in fact, live—and that because he will, the Philippians will have ample cause to celebrate and praise God as they await their reunion.

5. Why do you think Paul flips to this stance?

_____

_____

_____

_____

We don't know if the Lord suddenly gave Paul a beautiful revelation that he would, in fact, live or if Paul just decided to move forward with a positive outlook.

6. How would looking toward the positive help Paul in his current situation?

_____

_____

_____

_____

Admittedly, I roll my eyes when I hear the words *the power of positive thinking*—it just sounds so cliché and flimsy. But you know what *isn't* cliché and flimsy? Clinging to joy. And you know how we do that? By choosing to focus on the positive (what God can do) rather than on the negative (what might happen).

> *The pessimist sees difficulty in*
> *every opportunity. The optimist sees*
> *opportunity in every difficulty.*
> WINSTON CHURCHILL

I've always thought of myself as optimistic, but now that I'm married to an optimist, I realize how often I'm not. We've lived through some really hard stuff, so I know what *can* happen. It's hard for me, having experienced some worst-case scenarios, to look for the good and rest in trust. But I know that when I stop thinking about possibilities or dwelling on worst-case scenarios and instead truly rest in God's presence and power, God will lead me into joy. Not false, manufactured feelings—true, deep, tested joy. I have to be incredibly intentional about taking the joy Christ extends to me as a gift, but I'd rather persevere in the rest He calls me to than live in the anxiety of the what-ifs.

Ask God what it would look like to rest more intentionally so you're equipped to live in perseverance and tenaciously continue making a difference for the gospel.

Amen.

WEEK 2 • *Notes*

Share your biggest takeaways from this week:

Living Like Jesus

Philippians 1:27–2:18

WEEK 3 • *Day 1*

 READ PHILIPPIANS 1:27-30

Since high school, I'd wanted to dye my hair pink. Maybe because of Gwen Stefani's fabulous hair in her *No Doubt* days, or because Pink looked so gorgeous when she was still . . . well, pink. Or possibly watching *Grease* five thousand times had done it. Whatever the reason, two decades after high school, I found myself lamenting to my friend and hairstylist Kat that I'd missed "my window" for pink hair. After all, I was too old now to do something that silly, right?

Kat looked at me straight in the eyes through the big mirror in front of us and said, "Stop being timid. If you want pink hair, just do it. My mom is in her sixties and has bright purple hair! You're the only one saying you're too old."

When I left with a pink streak in my hair that day, I was crazy nervous. I wondered what people would think and was incredibly self-conscious. Yet every time I passed a mirror, the pink would catch my eye and I'd smile. I didn't do it for them. I did it for me.

About a year later, I was back in Kat's chair, gripping my coffee cup tightly as we went for it. After twenty years of wanting to, I went pink. All over pink. And then I freaked.

This was too bold, too crazy. I washed my hair five times that first day because I thought I looked like someone straight out of a comic book. I'm in leadership at church and travel around speaking at other churches. I had a big event with MOPS Corporate coming up mere days later. I didn't know how they'd all react, what they'd think of me. I got scared. What if people decided that a serious follower of Jesus couldn't possibly have pink hair?

That may seem like a roundabout way to get to our verses in Philippians today, but stick with me.

1. Write Philippians 1:27 here:

_____

_____

I was overwhelmingly afraid that the hue of my hair made me a poor example of what it means to follow Jesus. Would people look at me and think I wasn't smart and that I don't love Jesus as much as I do? But what does it really mean to let our manner of life be worthy of the gospel of Christ?

Here's what I had to learn: your hair, your tattoos, your piercings, your style—none of those things are about following Jesus. People judge us (and we judge each other!) over those kinds of things. But God tells us that He looks at the heart (1 Samuel 16:7).

Not everyone will like my pink hair, and that's fine . . . but the reality is that my hair has nothing to do with my love for Jesus or my commitment to following Him. So what does Paul mean by _conduct_ in this passage? Well, let's look at what Paul has said so far in Philippians that might give us an idea of what he means.

2. Reread where we've gone so far in Philippians 1. What does Paul indicate should define the life of a Jesus follower? (Hint: Check out Philippians 1:9-11 and 15-17 in particular.)

_____

_____

Our actions and way of living can either proclaim or detract from the Good News. When we sip a matcha latte at our favorite coffeehouse, push the cart at our neighborhood grocery store, walk down the hall at our workplace, or spend our Saturday mornings at the soccer field, we represent Christ. As we do these things and live through each day, we need to ask ourselves: Do we treat the people we come across and interact with in a manner worthy of the gospel?

- **Do we notice the people the world treats as invisible?** Beth Moore once shared about greeting and talking to the janitor in an airport restroom. The woman's eyes welled up with tears as she admitted that she would spend hours cleaning stalls and sinks, surrounded by women who don't even acknowledge her existence. Beth was the first one all day to say a single word to her and look her in the eye. Loving others means seeing them and acknowledging their God-given worth, no matter who they are.

- **Do we respond with grace when someone wrongs us?** Once, someone was totally road-raging at me because I accidentally cut them off. She raised a certain finger, rolled down her window to scream at me . . . it was a whole thing. It got super awkward when we pulled into the same parking lot and walked into church together. And I've totally been that girl, too, reacting badly when someone treats me in a way I don't think I deserve. Living out the gospel means squashing our angry reactions and allowing God's love to infuse our responses when we're wronged.

- **Do we bring humility instead of entitlement and pride when we disagree?** Social media provides some blatant and disgusting examples of how we treat one another. Somehow, sitting on the other side of a screen can give us false confidence and turn us into bullies. When we hear or read something we disagree with or don't like, choosing to hold our peace or respond respectfully speaks the truth of the gospel in a way dehumanizing words (even if they're preaching "truth"!) never can.

> *Burning down other's opinions*
> *doesn't make us right. It makes us arsonists.*[1]
>
> BOB GOFF

In the latter part of Philippians 1:27 and on into verse 28, Paul continues encouraging the Philippians to begin living in this manner now, not to wait for his return. And as they do, he wants them to stand firm with one mind, not being intimidated or frightened when others oppose them.

3. What do you think Paul intends when he says "one mind"?

4. Why might being "one mind" as God's people be so important, particularly in the face of opposition?

Paul is not saying that Christians should be mindless followers, but instead that we should walk together in pursuit of our main goal and focus: loving one another and upholding the mission of the gospel. Clarity and unity of purpose will keep us on track when we face opposition. (Notice that Paul doesn't say *if* we face opposition—when we follow Jesus, opposition is a foregone conclusion.)

When I talk about unity in the face of opposition, I'm not talking sticking together in anything and everything we might think makes a "good" Christian. Because there are a lot of things we might think fall under that category that aren't actually essential to our faith—and digging our heels in, expecting everyone else to agree with us, doesn't lead to unity. But being people of one mind in areas that are core to our faith—who Jesus is, why He came, the absolute need for His saving work on the cross to save us from our sins—means linking arms in unity, prioritizing love for others and trust in Jesus, no matter what we face.

5. What would it look like for you to stand firm when you face opposition for your love of Christ and belief in the gospel?

_____

_____

_____

_____

6. How might opposition benefit us and our faith in Christ?

_____

_____

_____

_____

Although my family moved around a bit when I was growing up, I attended mostly Christian schools and lived in a little bubble of mostly like-minded people. Then, in my junior year of high school, my parents put me in a public school for the first time since I was little. As much as I wouldn't have admitted it at the time, it was one of the best parenting decisions they ever made. Being surrounded by kids who didn't love Jesus grounded me in my faith because for the first time in my life, I had to stand up for what I believed. Instead of sitting comfortably alongside Christian friends, I was mocked and made fun of for my faith. With every snicker, every mean or back-handed comment, every party invitation, I had to decide if I would truly stand up _for_ Him and stand _with_ Him. I certainly wasn't perfect, but eventually the mocking and snide comments slowed as people recognized I lived what I believed and wasn't trying to cram it down anyone else's throat.

Comfort can lead to complacency, but opposition can strengthen us because we're forced to live out what we say we believe. And as we stand firm in the face of opposition, we see God meet us and sustain us in the midst of it.

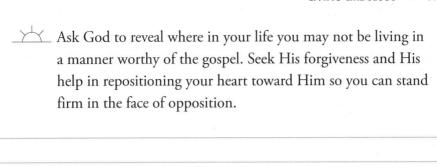 Ask God to reveal where in your life you may not be living in a manner worthy of the gospel. Seek His forgiveness and His help in repositioning your heart toward Him so you can stand firm in the face of opposition.

Amen.

WEEK 3 ● *Day 2*

 READ PHILIPPIANS 2:1-4

This morning I heard one of our dogs run downstairs extra early, so I pushed back my covers, followed her down, and opened the back door to let her out. As I went to the kitchen to make some coffee, I smiled because I realized what day it is. Sunday is my favorite day because we have church—but today is particularly fun because we're having International Food Night.

Our community that gathers to worship together every weekend is sort of a motley crew, which is a perfect picture of the big, beautiful body of Christ. We're a group of toddlers and teenagers and singles and millennials and retirees. We're white and not white. Some of us speak English as a first language, and some of us speak a different language at home. We're ex-gang members, felons, ex-missionaries, and straight-laced businessmen and women.

International Food Night is a favorite of mine because my parents did me right and taught me to love our world's rich variety of food. Dark sauces steeped for days so the flavor has just the right intensity. Garlicky vegetables blanched with ingredients you can only find in that culture's local market (or brought straight from someone's homeland!). Coriander, turmeric, cardamom. Leafy greens, root vegetables, beans, melons, and mushrooms. Fresh-pressed olive oil, rosemary, and capers. Tonight our church is united not only by the love of Jesus but also by the love of community and unity through the flavors of our upbringing.

Reading today's passage about unity and fellowship makes me think that Paul would have liked our church, though we're still learning exactly what unity amidst diversity means, just like your church probably is. Because you know what? Unity matters. Diversity matters. Community and fellowship matter. These things matter because they remind us how Jesus created His people to be living examples of His love. I think *The Message* perfectly captures the essence of what Paul is saying here:

> If you've gotten anything at all out of following Christ, if his love has made any difference in your life, if being in a community of the Spirit means anything to you, if you have a heart, if you *care*—then do me a favor: Agree with each other, love each other, be deep-spirited friends. Don't push your way to the front; don't sweet-talk your way to the top. Put yourself aside, and help others get ahead. Don't be obsessed with getting your own advantage. Forget yourselves long enough to lend a helping hand.
>
> PHILIPPIANS 2:1-4

We all learned about cause and effect as children, right? *If* we throw the ball at the window, *then* it will break. *If* we jump on the trampoline, *then* it will bounce. When we see an *if*, a *then* should be close by because you cannot have one without the other, sort of like peanut butter and jelly. And we see a lot of *ifs* in the first part of these verses!

1. List out all of Paul's *ifs* in this passage (I'll do the first one):

if. . . you've gotten anything at all out of following Christ

if. . . _____

if. . . _____

if. . . _____

if. . . _____

Paul's *thens* that follow the *ifs* point us to the way we come together in unity as God's people: *then do me a favor*, or *then make my joy complete*. How do we fulfill the *thens*? By doing and *not* doing certain things.

2. Using Paul's words in Philippians 2:1-4, list what we should and shouldn't do as we pursue unity:

DO THESE THINGS	DON'T DO THESE THINGS

3. When looking at the "Do these things" column, *star* the one that feels easiest for you to do, and *circle* the one that you struggle with most.

4. What makes the starred one simple to do? When have you done it?

_____

_____

_____

_____

_____

5. What makes the circled one difficult to do? When have you avoided doing it?

_____

_____

_____

_____

Paul knew unity was critical for the body of Christ because our unity displays the legitimacy of the gospel. Loving one another well and seeking to be one in Christ amidst all our differences shows our hearts. However—and this is important—unity doesn't just happen simply because we love Jesus. Cultivating unity takes effort, obedience, and intentionality.

6. Philippians 2:1-4 and Philippians 1:27 both seem to be talking about being one as the body of Christ—but how are these passages different?

_____

_____

_____

Let's jump back into Philippians 1:27 and look at the BLB for a minute. As we scroll down within the *Interlinear* section for this verse, we see that Paul uses the phrase *you are standing firm* or *stēkō* (στήκω, pronounced *stay-ko*). This means "to stand firm," "to persevere, to persist," and "to keep one's standing."[2] I really like how this phrase is described farther down, in the *Thayer's Greek Lexicon*.

7. Scroll down to the *Thayer's Greek Lexicon* and write out the words listed in bold:

_____

_____

_____

Those bolded words say things like "to keep one's standing," "not to sin," and "to stand erect." If we dig in deeper and read the lightface text within *Thayer's Greek Lexicon*, we'll see it also says "to persevere in godliness and rectitude [uprightness and integrity] in one's fellowship with the Lord."[3] Paul is explaining that if we're to stand side by side, we need to be people who are internally healthy and walking close to Christ. In other words, if we're unhealthy inwardly, we're unable to be unified outwardly. Makes sense, right?

At the end of Philippians 1:27, Paul encourages a unity of minds ("with one mind striving side by side for the faith of the gospel"), as we talked about yesterday. In Philippians 2:1-4, he's emphasizing this unity of mind, but he speaks about it within a larger spirit of love ("having the same love").

8. What do you think it means to have the same love?

_____

_____

_____

God created each of us as unique individuals, and we celebrate the fact that we all look different, act differently, and enjoy doing different things. I can love wearing heels, skiing, and staying up way too late reading . . . and you can dislike every single one of those things. We can be hard-core committed to various products and thought processes. We can hold different political views and value different theological perspectives. These kinds of differences are not what Paul is talking about here as he encourages us to have one mind and the same love. Instead, Paul is encouraging us to have the same love for one another that Christ has for us. We need to literally be like-souled, one in spirit as we step out as a people with one purpose: loving Jesus, loving others, and sharing that love with everyone we meet.

Share with the Lord any struggles you have in loving people who may not think like you, look like you, or even love Jesus like you do. Ask for His mind and heart to be your mind and heart so you can love them like He does.

Amen.

WEEK 3 • *Day 3*

 READ PHILIPPIANS 2:5-11

Paul proclaims a glorious truth in today's Scripture: Jesus came from the paradise of heaven down to earth, leaving the physicality of His high position without giving up the authority and reality of who He is. He was every bit still God, even while in human form.

The whole concept of being 100 percent human and still 100 percent God will forever boggle my mind. Nothing about Jesus emptying Himself, "taking the form of a servant [who was] born in the likeness of men" (Philippians 2:7) has changed the reality that He is still God.

That phrase "emptied himself" sticks out to me, because it reminds me of a recent conversation with a friend. She admitted that she gives and gives and has nothing left—particularly for herself. As women, don't we often find ourselves in that place? We empty ourselves for the sake of the people around us, and we find ourselves drained and burned out as a result. I have to remind myself how crucial it is to protect myself from that kind of emptying because none of us can pour from an empty cup. When we pour ourselves out, we are completely tapped and quite honestly not effective or good for anything. For some reason, we think self-care or even soul care is a luxury not meant for every day.

1. Do you struggle with burnout—with pouring yourself out for the sake of the people in your life, to the point that you feel empty and ineffective? Do you see that as healthy or unhealthy?

So what does it mean that Christ actually *did* pour Himself out? If it's not healthy or wise for us to pour ourselves out, because we'll be completely emptied and unable to ultimately care for anyone, including ourselves, then why does Paul point us to the example of Jesus, who emptied Himself on our behalf?

2. Let's do some digging. Please tap on Philippians 2:7 in the BLB and click on the *Interlinear*. What does the word *emptied* (*kenoō*; κενόω, pronounced *ke-no-oh*) mean?

"To make empty," "to . . . hollow," and even "[laying] aside equality" and "render[ing] vain, useless."[4] Do you feel like this definition helped at all? Not really, huh? Hmm . . . well, what if we're not finding a helpful answer because we're asking the wrong question?

What if rather than asking, *What did Christ empty Himself of?* we need to inquire, *What did He empty Himself into?*

3. What do you think is the difference between these two questions?

Jesus didn't empty Himself of His deity so that He no longer contained it. God is not a finite being like we are, where there is an end to what He can pour out—He is endless fullness. And He did not empty Himself into a void. Instead, Jesus spilled all His glorious divinity *into* humanity and into the form of a man—becoming fully God and fully human at the same time. I know, this is a hard one to understand. I don't think anyone could ever fully comprehend it.

Jesus was poured out, but not in the way we think of it. As one of my favorite commentaries says, "He laid aside his glory in the view of men, not by lessening it, but by concealing it."[5]

Paul's beautiful words here are essentially a theologically dense *CliffsNotes* version of the gospel itself: who Jesus is, why He came, what He did, and what His work means. This passage is often called the *Christ Hymn* or the *Messiah Poem* and can be broken into three sections.

4. How would you divide up the three sections? Please draw a line from each segment of verses to the appropriate description:

Philippians 2:6-7	the glorification and exaltation of Christ
Philippians 2:8	the true character of the Godhead
Philippians 2:9-11	the incarnation (personification) of Jesus Himself

5. Why do you think Paul included this gospel message and hymn in his letter to the believers in Philippi?

This hymn is written directly after Paul's exhortation for unity in Philippians 2:1-4. We have to remember that every encouragement, challenge, prayer, and comment in this letter flows in and out of what came before and what follows. Nothing stands alone.

6. Please write down Philippians 2:5.

Prior to sharing this theologically dense version of the gospel in Philippians 2:6-11, Paul reminds them to be united in heart and mind (verse 5). Unity requires an example, a picture of what they are aiming for. Paul wants them, rather than desiring power and control and looking at one another in competition, to look toward Christ as the ultimate example of living with a spirit of unity, humility, love, and servanthood.

7. How could you use this gospel message from the *Christ Hymn* as a reminder and encouragement as you seek unity too?

_____

_____

_____

_____

_____

 ### *History Lesson*

In the Roman Empire, Caesar was Lord[6]—and because of that, Rome was not a big fan of Jesus being worshiped as the One True God. Proclaiming Jesus as Lord directly opposed the religion of the day. At the time Paul wrote this letter to the Philippian church, the city of Philippi was home to an imperial cult that centered around worshiping Caesar Augustus, his wife Livia, and their grandson Claudius. Within this cult, it was taught that Caesar and his family would rise as gods after their deaths.

In Philippians 2:5-11, Paul may have used the word *kenosis* (emptying) instead of *apotheosis* (immortalization) to remind his Philippian friends how their beliefs differed from the teaching and culture that surrounded them. Paul made the distinction clear: Humans don't become gods; God became a human.[7]

Some parts of the Bible won't fully make sense to us because our minds cannot grasp the magnitude of who God is. That's how I feel about this passage in Philippians. I understand the basis of what's being said—that Christ emptied Himself out and that even as He did so, His divinity remained in all its fullness. But how can someone be empty and full at the same time?

The closest comparison I can make is the love I have for my family. I pour out that love to them every day—and yet the level of it never decreases. It's not a perfect analogy, but it gives me a glimpse into the mystery—and the beauty—of it all. There is no end to who God is, no end to His divinity and power and authority, and no end to His mercy and grace and love. And that is very good news indeed.

Talk to God about the things about Him you find hard to comprehend. Ask Him to give you the faith and trust to live in mystery and to deepen your desire to know Him more.

Amen.

WEEK 3 • *Day 4*

 READ PHILIPPIANS 2:12-13

You know what's a big deal to me? When someone knows my coffee order. I feel like that's the ultimate intimacy in friendship—when someone values me enough to pay attention to the little things. The little things are what make us feel known.

We all like feeling known, but what are we known *for*? Last night, we held our monthly women's event at church, and one of the women sharing her testimony mentioned that she used to be known as the one you want to go out with if you're looking to party. Another girl who opened up talked about dealing with depression after being raped. She told us that she couldn't even open her Bible in that season. She said, "And any of you who know me will get that me not reading my Bible is megaweird. If I'm not reading it daily, you know I'm in a bad spot."

What about you and me? We may be known as a pessimist or an optimist. We might be known for being patient or hotheaded. Maybe we're known for volunteering, for giving great advice, for keeping a beautiful home, or for being involved in politics.

1. What are you known for?

_____

_____

_____

2. Think back on what we've covered so far in these past three weeks. What was the church in Philippi known for?

_____

_____

_____

In Philippians 2:12, we see that one of the main things this body of believers is known for is their obedience to Christ. And what about that word Paul puts before *obeyed*? *Always*. Seriously? They *always obeyed*? Yikes—that definitely doesn't apply to me. What about you? Would you be considered *always* obedient to Christ?

Because I was having a hard time wrapping my mind around this idea of people always being obedient to Christ, I opened up the BLB. When I clicked on the phrase *you have always* or *pantote* (πάντοτε, pronounced *pahn-toe-tey*) to double-check, I saw that sure enough, *pantote* literally means "at all times, always, ever(more)."[8]

But before you start freaking out that you can never live up to that level of perfection, let's consider something. Paul knows just as well as you and I do that no one is perfect except God Himself. So he is likely making a general statement that this group knows they're supposed to obey Him and live in consistent *pursuit* of that obedience—not that they're steeped in a life of unattainable perfection.

3. What about Paul's friends in Philippi reveals their pattern of obedience? (Hint: You might have to flip through our previous days or skim Philippians 1:5 and 1:19 as a reminder.)

Let's back up a minute and look at the first word in Philippians 2:12. My ESV Bible translates it as *therefore*. And—if you grew up attending Sunday school or a church youth group, you may know this ditty—whenever we see the word *therefore*, we need to ask ourselves what it's *there for*.

4. What is the word *therefore* there for in Philippians 2:12?

When we look back to Philippians 2:1-11, we read about following the example of Christ Jesus. Verse 8 even talks about His obedience:

And being found in human form, he humbled himself by becoming obedient to the point of death, even death on a cross.

PHILIPPIANS 2:8

Sometimes I think we forget that Jesus was 100 percent man and thus 100 percent freaking out at the idea of being put to death— particularly death on a cross, which meant excruciating pain, shame, and torture. He even begged God the Father for another way (Matthew 26:39). And yet Jesus still obeyed.

When Paul says *therefore* in Philippians 2:12, he is pointing back to Jesus' example. Jesus obeyed God all the way to the cross, *therefore* the Philippians should continue in their obedience. But he also reminds them (and us) that we don't do this on our own.

5. Please write down verse 13 below:

God works in us, equipping us to continue in obedience! Knowing that we depend on God to help us obey and follow Him should keep us from becoming complacent. Even when we feel like we're doing well, we need to "work out [our] own salvation with fear and trembling" (Philippians 2:12). Paul may be acknowledging the

Philippians' ongoing obedience, but we see in the rest of the letter that they face many obstacles: disunity (2:14; 4:2-3), false teachers (3:2-4), Christ haters (3:18). Since humility is a theme throughout the letter, the Philippians may have been battling an attitude of pride.

Paul encourages his Philippian friends to continue in their obedience because he doesn't want to assume that their past good work in following God would automatically translate into sustained excellence in faith and obedience. Equally, our relationship with God should be ongoing as we grow in humility and dependence on Him.

Ask God to unearth the places where He wants to refine you, so that you may be increasingly known for your love and obedience to Him.

Amen.

WEEK 3 • *Day 5*

  READ PHILIPPIANS 2:14-18

Have you ever used the phrase *all the things*? You know the one: Drink coffee and do all the things. Go to Target and buy all the things. Make all the things, organize all the things, watch all the things, eat all the things. And apparently even Paul liked that phrase! (Okay, okay—maybe he was missing the word *the*. Minor detail.)

Paul's "all the things," though, feels like a pretty tall order. Philippians 2:14 says to do all things . . .

- "without grumbling or disputing";
- "readily and cheerfully—no bickering, no second-guessing" (MSG); and
- "without complaining or division among yourselves" (TPT).

1. Let's dig into this concept of grumbling in the BLB. *Grumbling* (*goggysmos*; γογγυσμός, pronounced *gon-goose-mas*) can also be translated as . . .

This is officially my favorite Greek word because it just rolls off my tongue and sounds awesome. I've started saying, "Guys! No *gon-goose-mas!*" whenever my kids are griping about something. They roll their eyes and don't get why I love saying it. But hey, they're too busy making fun of me to grumble . . . so, you know, mom win!

My kids *goggysmos* about taking the dogs on a walk before school. They *goggysmos* when it's time for bed and when it's time to get up in the morning. And . . . let's be honest: They're not the only ones who *goggysmos*. Right now, I'm grumbling about them grumbling! I *goggysmos* a lot—while paying bills, while stuck in traffic, while cleaning up something that spilled that no one else bothered to clean up. I grumble about taking the puppy out. I *goggysmos* while folding laundry, putting away laundry (actually, pretty much anything to do with laundry) . . .

2. Where does grumbling pop up in your life?

_____

_____

_____

_____

Maybe you're not the type of person to internally grumble about things throughout the day. But the reality is, we all have things that get under our skin and tempt us to grumble. And we can justify it, right? Sometimes the kids are frustrating, or our boss doesn't recognize us for all that extra work we did, or our friends forgot our birthday. Grumbling can feel earned and cathartic. But Paul is saying here in Philippians that no matter what, and *in all things*, we are not to grumble. Can we make a conscious effort to stop? Can we make a conscious effort to *do all the things* with a joyful heart?

3. How are we supposed to do all things without grumbling? (Hint: Check out Philippians 2:14-18.)

_____

_____

_____

Did you find it? If you're studying out of the ESV like I am, you'll see that Philippians 2:18 says to be "glad and rejoice." Through our study so far, we've already hit on this concept several times. We are to turn our eyes toward the blessings and *eucharisteō* (Philippians 1:3-8) in everything we do. We are to position ourselves toward the positive rather than the negative (Philippians 1:24-26).

4. Why are we to do these things and turn away from grumbling, bickering, and negativity? (Hint: See Philippians 2:15.)

My ESV translates Paul's reasoning for not grumbling as: "that you may be blameless and innocent, children of God without blemish in the midst of a crooked and twisted generation, among whom you shine as lights in the world."

I love how *The Message* translates it too: "Provide people with a glimpse of good living and of the living God. Carry the light-giving Message into the night."

5. Using the BLB or focusing on the heart of what Paul is saying, rewrite verse 15 in your own words.

6. Why is this message so important to Paul? (Hint: See verse 16.)

Paul wants the truth of the gospel to be spread throughout Rome, Philippi, and the entire world. He wants believers to be known for being light in a dark world. When the Philippians stay away from a posture of grumbling and disputing, they will act as striking representatives of Jesus—which, for Paul, means that all his work won't have been in vain. Even while he is in prison, and even if he is approaching the end of his life, the Good News of Jesus will continue to spread because of the example of those who follow Him.

We each have an opportunity to carry the light-giving Message out of life's darkness and into the light. Let's be known for being different—for loving people well, for choosing kindness and joy instead of grumbling and division. This doesn't mean being happy-go-lucky or dismissing the very real pain and struggle we face. We can live out a deep, rich, textural kind of love and joy, which emerges through depending on God amid every circumstance.

> ¹⁶ Cling to the word of life so that on the day of judgment when the Anointed One returns I may have reason to rejoice, because it will be plain that I didn't turn from His mission nor did I work in vain. ¹⁷ Even if my lifeblood is to be poured out like wine as a sacrifice of your faith, I have great reason to celebrate with all of you. ¹⁸ And for the same reason, you can be glad and celebrate with me.
>
> PHILIPPIANS 2:16-18, VOICE

Approach the throne in humility, asking God to convict you of the things you *goggysmos* about. Then, write a long list of all the things you're thankful for. Thank the Lord for each blessing that pours from your pen to the paper—big or small.

Amen.

WEEK 3 • *Notes*

Share your biggest takeaways from this week:

Rising Up

Philippians 2:19-30

WEEK 4 • *Day 1*

 READ PHILIPPIANS 2:19-24 & ACTS 14

We've been talking about the building blocks of a life that really matters—pursuing unity, avoiding grumbling, being living examples of the Good News of Jesus. But you know who I bet lived that kind of life? Timothy. We get a glimpse of how Paul feels about this young man, and it's pretty incredible. Not only were they friends and brothers in Christ, but Paul considered him family, like the son he never had. Timothy must have been quite the guy because I feel like Paul is kind of a hard sell, don't you? He and Timothy must have had quite the backstory—and that's where we're going to start today. Understanding the backstory will help us when we dive into these verses tomorrow.

In Acts 14, we learn that Paul and Barnabas were sharing the gospel in a town called Iconium. But they soon realized that a group of unbelieving Jews were poisoning the minds of the Gentiles against the message of Jesus. This anti-Jesus group was so venomous and convincing, they were able to turn both the leaders of the city and the townspeople against the Good News of Jesus. Paul and Barnabas fled the city after catching wind of a plot to stone them (Acts 14:1-7).

 History Lesson

ICONIUM

Are you a fan of Greek mythology? Some of my kids are learning about it in school right now. The city *Iconium* got its name from the root word *eikon*, the Greek word for "image." That word connects to Greek mythology, when after a great flood (likely inspired by Noah's flood) the gods Prometheus and

Athena formed human images from mud and breathed life into them.[1] Known for its beautiful gardens, the thriving city of Iconium was set right in the midst of farms and orchards, though it was surrounded by deserts. Iconium was located along the main trade route between Ephesus and Syria and the Mesopotamian world, which contributed to the hustle and bustle of industry as well as orchard and farm enterprises.[2]

LYSTRA

The Roman colony of Lystra (modern-day Zoldera) was the furthest east of all the fortified cities of Galatia. Since a typical day's journey in the Roman Empire during this time was twenty miles, the city of Lystra easily became the market town of Lycaonia (south-central modern-day Turkey) because it was only about twenty miles south of Iconium.

Luke did not mention evangelizing at the synagogue while Paul preached at this market city, and because of this, we can speculate that, as in Philippi, the Jewish population there was likely too small to warrant a synagogue.[3] Instead, a temple dedicated to Zeus resided near the gates of the city. The city was also home to a statue of Hermes.

We wouldn't consider Lystra a particularly strategic place for Paul to take the gospel—it was not an important trading or manufacturing center. But think again! Lystra resided in the heart of the agricultural region of Turkey. The people hearing the Good News of Jesus would have been farmers, people who made their living from the soil. This reminds us that the gospel was for everyone—from the elite guards in Rome to the everyday people in rural towns.

After Paul and Barnabas left Iconium, they arrived in Lystra. While there, they met a man who had been crippled from birth, and Paul healed him. We learn that this man immediately "sprang up and began walking" (Acts 14:10)! In Greek, the word translated as *sprang up* is *hallomai* (ἅλλομαι, pronounced *hahl-lo-mai*) and literally means "to leap," "to jump," "to gush up: of water."[4] I love this visual. Can't you just see this man springing up onto his now-healed feet, jumping and dancing around? In biblical times, people looked at illness, impairment, and irregularity as a curse from God or the gods (John 9:2)—so this would have simply boggled their minds!

But then things started to get weird. The superstitious townspeople suddenly believed that Paul and Barnabas were Hermes and Zeus and shouted in Lycaonian, "The gods have come down to us in the likeness of men!" (Acts 14:11). Then they tried to sacrifice offerings to Paul and Barnabas, who of course tried to tell them who they really were and why they were really there. Yet verse 18 tells us, "Even with these words they scarcely restrained the people from offering sacrifice to them."

Can you imagine Paul and Barnabas trying to get a word in edgewise as the excited townsfolk were exclaiming their glory and bringing them things in honor and sacrifice? The two men probably looked at each other with wide eyes as they shrugged and continued trying to explain who had healed this man. It wouldn't be the last time Paul was seen as a god because of miraculous healing (see Acts 28). But every single time, Paul immediately pointed people back to Christ.

1. How could you develop a more intentional habit of pointing back to Jesus' work in the midst of things you might be tempted to take credit for?

It can be so easy to lean so much on using our own abilities and knowledge that our first instinct when something good happens is to be self-proud, self-appreciative, or self-focused. But we see from Paul's example that everything we go through should illuminate Jesus and draw others to Him. We are the illustration; He is the story.

Even if Paul had been tempted to take credit for the miracle, the crowd was unpredictable. While they started off celebrating Paul and Barnabas, they quickly changed their minds once angry Jews from Antioch and Iconium entered the city, looking for these men who had escaped them. We don't know exactly what these Jews said to turn the tide against Paul and Barnabas, but we do know the result: Paul was dragged out of the city, stoned, and left for dead. In fact, he was so unresponsive, everyone thought he *was* dead! After the angry crowd dissipated, the disciples (*mathētēs*; μαθητής, pronounced *math-ay-tays*) gathered around him (likely praying) and Paul rose up. Not only was he not dead . . . but he was healed enough to get up and walk!

> *Note:* Disciples *or* mathētēs *simply means a learner, pupil, someone who follows one's teaching. This is not to be confused with the specific group of Jesus' closest confidants, the twelve disciples.*

2. What did Paul immediately do after this near-death stoning? (Hint: See verse 20.)

Paul had every right to walk away from Lystra at this point. But he didn't. Maybe he entered back through the city gates under the protection of darkness. Or perhaps it was still daylight, and the crowd, amazed that he was alive, parted silently as he walked through. Whatever the case, Paul wasn't done with Lystra. Even though he left the next day, he returned after preaching the gospel in Derbe:

> [21] When they had preached the gospel to that city [Derbe] and had made many disciples, they returned to Lystra and to Iconium and to Antioch, [22] strengthening the souls of the disciples, encouraging them to continue in the faith, and saying that through many tribulations we must enter the kingdom of God. [23] And when they had appointed elders for them in every church, with prayer and fasting they committed them to the Lord in whom they had believed.
>
> ACTS 14:21-23

3. According to Acts 14:21-23, what was Paul's aim in returning to these churches?

   a. _____

   b. _____

   c. _____

   d. _____

   e. _____

Five-ish years later, Paul returned to Lystra and Iconium for a third time to check on the churches that had been established there. It was during this third visit (his second missionary journey) that he met Timothy (Acts 16).

4. How do you think Paul's commitment to the believers in Lystra may have affected Timothy?

5. What does the New Testament tell us about Timothy?

Acts 16:1

Acts 16:2

Acts 16:3

2 Timothy 1:5

6. Based on what we've learned, what kind of man do you think
   Timothy was?

The only thing we know about Timothy's father is that he was
Greek. But we know much more about his mother and grandmother,

who must have been incredible women. Paul identifies them by name, highlighting their faith as the foundation for Timothy's own relationship with God. Eunice and Lois were likely early converts who helped shape the church in Lystra.[5] And from the time Timothy was a child, these two women invested in a young man who would play a significant role in spreading the message of Jesus.

By agreeing to be circumcised, Timothy demonstrated immense commitment to Christ and a desire to be effective as he joined Paul in his missionary journeys. We know from Galatians that Paul didn't think non-Jewish Christians needed be circumcised, but he also knew that Timothy's Greek heritage could be an obstacle for Jews who needed to hear the gospel. Circumcision was a tangible way for Timothy to build trust and credibility with the Jewish community.

Paul's experiences in and around Lystra were painful and traumatic. But do you think the struggle and pain was worth it to Paul? Because Paul was faithful to the believers in Lystra, he gained a son in the faith who would remain one of his closest friends until the end of his life. If we find ourselves in an especially hard season, let's be encouraged by Paul and Timothy: God might be creating something extraordinary in the darkness.

Think of the women in your life who have shaped you and your faith. Thank the Lord for them today and pray that you, too, could be used for God's glory in the lives of other women. Whom could you mentor and love intentionally?

Amen.

WEEK 4 • *Day 2*

 READ PHILIPPIANS 2:19-24

I love Dr. Seuss. In fact, I love his books more now when I read them to my children than I did as a little girl. Now that I'm older, I'm able to see the deeper message beneath the whimsy of these stories.

I graduated with a degree in art history, not just because I love art but because I love backstory. I love to know why an artist painted this or sculpted that. I love to learn about the symbolism and hidden meaning—and what was going on in society or culture that inspired a creation. And with Dr. Seuss, I love knowing that *Horton Hears a Who* is about equality and that *Green Eggs and Ham* was written as a bet between Dr. Seuss and his editor to prove that he could write a meaningful early-reader book using fifty or fewer words.[6]

That's why backstory is such a big deal to me when I'm studying the Bible. Everything is so much richer when I read it with the understanding that the gospel is the thread stringing the entirety of Scripture together—and that there are no one-off stories. Everything in God's Word is woven together and interconnected.

Yesterday we stepped out of Philippians to dive into the backstory of Timothy's hometown of Lystra, and today we're going to flip around a bit inside Philippians to talk about what a man of rare character Timothy was, how selfless he was in loving others, and how we can absorb these things into our own lives and hearts.

1. Quickly head back to Philippians 1:1. Who was the letter to the Philippians from? (Hint: If you're not even flipping back to look because you're rolling your eyes and saying, "Paul. Duh," then you're only half right.)

Paul included Timothy in the greeting of this letter, which is interesting because Timothy didn't write it—not even a portion of it. In fact, we know it's written solely by Paul and not a Paul/Timothy combination because if we do a word search (in ESV), we'll see the word *we* only three times, while the word *I* appears over forty times.

Timothy may be included because Paul has such high esteem for his second-in-command. Timothy is Paul's proxy (1 Corinthians 4:16-17; 1 Thessalonians 3:2-3), and because Paul included Timothy's name at the beginning of the letter (Philippians 1:1), we know that Timothy was physically with him. Timothy, along with another man named Epaphroditus (whom we'll learn about tomorrow), voluntarily lived in the rented home where Paul stayed under house arrest. Timothy may have been the one who transcribed the letter as Paul dictated it in chains, or perhaps he was simply on Paul's heart and mind as he wrote the message to his friends in Philippi. But as we learn in today's reading, Paul intends for Timothy to leave him and go to Philippi.

In verse 20, Paul says that he has no one like Timothy because he is of kindred spirit and is genuinely concerned about others. This word *concerned* or *merimnaō* (μεριμνάω, pronounced *me-rim-nah-o*) means "to be troubled with cares," "to care for, look out for," "to seek to promote one's interests."[7]

2. If, as Paul says, Timothy is the only one who is looking out for the benefit of others, what is everyone else doing? (Hint: See verse 21.)

3. How does Philippians 2:4 help us understand Philippians 2:21?

Let each of you look not only to his own interests, but also to the interests of others.

PHILIPPIANS 2:4

For they all seek their own interests, not those of Jesus Christ.

PHILIPPIANS 2:21

Timothy is others-first, others-minded. He lives in a way that is in step with the gospel and adheres to what Paul was encouraging in Philippians 1:27-28. He looks not to his own interests, he looks to the interests of others, and he seeks the interests of Jesus Christ.

4. Are you doing these three things in your own life right now? How would you like to grow in this area?

Paul has talked about unity over and over in our time together. He believes that we achieve unity when we lay aside selfish ambition (Philippians 2:3-4). We must prioritize community and collaboration over competition. We need to live an others-oriented life.

Pursuing true joy doesn't conflict with considering others' interests in a life of unity and fearlessness. We find joy when we live a *selfless*, others-oriented life (as we see in Paul's words in Philippians 2:2 and 2:19).

5. Who do you know who exemplifies this kind of life? What does that look like?

Timothy evidently adheres to and lives the life that Paul tells the Philippians is essential to their flourishing. If Jesus' example feels unattainable, we should look at Timothy, too, because he's an everyday person living out the life that matters.

As we wrap up our time together today, talk to the Lord about becoming a woman who truly loves all people all the time (or, as Bob Goff would say, "Everybody always"!). This is how we truly create a life that matters.

God wants me to love the ones I don't understand, to get to know their names. To invite them to do things with me. To go and find the ones everyone has shunned and turned away. To see them as my neighbors even if we are in totally different places. You'll be able to spot people who are becoming love because they want to build kingdoms, not castles. They fill their lives with people who don't look like them or act like them or even believe the same things as them. They treat them with love and respect and are more eager to learn from them than presume they have something to teach.[8]

BOB GOFF

Amen.

WEEK 4 ● *Day 3*

 READ PHILIPPIANS 2:25-27

Has a random compliment ever stuck with you? One time when I was playing in my farmor's hat collection as a child, my dad said I look great in hats . . . and now I have a whole shelf of them. In high school, someone told me they loved my laugh because it made them laugh—and I continue to pursue a life filled with laughter.

Life-giving words breathe encouragement into our spirits and can have an impact that goes far beyond the words themselves. Words of life move us to action, calling us to become people who are more like Jesus. And often, those words don't have to be directed to us—they can be about people who inspire us and call us to follow Jesus more passionately. We see a vivid example of that in today's passage.

Although Paul was a straight shooter, he was also life-giving. And he's not just *telling* us the way to life, he's *showing* us what that kind of life looks like. Paul spoke life into Timothy, developing him into a leader who loved God and loved others. We see in Timothy's life what it looks like to follow Jesus' example while living in unity and boldness. And today, Paul introduces us to another man we can learn from: Epaphroditus.

1. Write down all the ways Paul describes Epaphroditus in Philippians 2:25:

_____

_____

_____

_____

_____

Talk about a man with a bunch of jobs! Brother, fellow worker, fellow soldier, messenger, minister. I find this Epaphroditus guy so relatable. I, too, feel like I have about a million job titles: mom, wife, taxi driver, cook, counselor, housekeeper, professional snuggler and tucker-inner, writer, Bible teacher, speaker, friend, mentor, and on and on. I'll bet you have your own endless list. So, how do we become women who are essential in the work of the Lord—even while wearing 1,001 hats?

Let's dig into each of Epaphroditus's five jobs, using the *Interlinear* for this passage in the BLB. I'll do the last three for you, but for the first two, write down the meanings you find in the provided lines:

2. *Brother* (*adelphos*; ἀδελφός, pronounced *ah-del-fos*)

Obviously, these men are not literal brothers but are united through the bond of Christ and have sworn loyalty and friendship to each other. Paul thinks of Epaphroditus as family, an important part of his tribe and his team. Epaphroditus is loved and needed, essential in the life of Paul the person, not just Paul the missionary, teacher, and preacher.

Paul's friendship with Epaphroditus is massively significant. Remember Paul's history? He was a Pharisee and would never have had any interaction with a Gentile, on whom the Pharisees look down, before becoming a follower of Jesus. But Paul now understands that the Good News of Jesus is for all people and that everyone who follows Jesus is his brother and sister, no matter their origin or descent.

3. *Fellow worker* (*synergos*; συνεργός, pronounced *soon-er-gos*)

You may have noticed that the Greek word is where our English word *synergy* comes from. If you looked up the word *synergy* in an English dictionary, you'd see that it's defined as "the interaction or cooperation of two or more organizations, substances, or other agents to produce a combined effect greater than the sum of their separate effects."[9]

This definition of synergy helps me understand why unity was so important to Paul. We are made for community, and community in the body of Christ amplifies our work in ways we could never do on our own. We see an incredible example of that here, as Epaphroditus worked alongside Paul, furthering the cause for Christ even as Paul was in chains.

4. Have you seen synergy in a relationship or partnership? What did you learn from that experience?

Epaphroditus gave up his own independence to live with Paul while he was imprisoned. How many people would you do that for? Would you travel thousands of miles from your home to move into a place where a friend was imprisoned, trading everything familiar and safe in order to share the gospel . . . in order to care for a friend in need? In all likelihood, Epaphroditus (and Timothy) preached on Paul's behalf and carried messages to people and to church groups. These men would have been Paul's hands and feet when he wasn't permitted to leave his home.

A few years ago, my best friend Kiesha's husband called me to tell me that she'd had a stroke. It was only weeks after their first child was born, and Kiesha would be in a hospital several hours away from their home. David was trying to figure out how on earth he could take care of both their tiny infant and his ailing wife. I booked a flight that day and flew out that very evening, spending a blissful week with a newborn I still refer to as "my baby" five years later. Kiesha faced a long road to recovery, and our little group of friends tag-teamed, each taking a week with the baby until a family member could take over.

When our friends are hurting, we want to be there for them. And they'd do the same for us. That's what we see from Epaphroditus here: He's risking his own life and comfort for both Paul and the gospel.

5. Do you have friends you'd lay down everything for? What would it look like for you to commit to be with someone through thick and thin, casting aside your comfort out of love for them?

Epaphroditus's three other jobs seem closely related to the first two—tying together both his close relationship with Paul and his desire to preach the gospel:

- *Fellow soldier* (*systratiōtēs*; συστρατιώτης, pronounced *su-strah-tee-oh-tays*): "a fellow soldier," "an associate in labours and conflicts for the cause of Christ," "an associate in Christian toil"[10]

- *Messenger* (*apostolos*; ἀπόστολος, pronounced *ah-pos-tol-os*): "a messenger," "a delegate," "an ambassador of the Gospel," "officially a commissioner of Christ ('apostle')."[11]

- *Minister (to my need)* (*leitourgos*; λειτουργός, pronounced *lay-toor-gos*): "a public minister, a servant of the state," "a servant of the temple," "one busied with holy things"[12]

Tomorrow we're going to explore Epaphroditus's *minister* hat, but before we end our time together today, I want to point out an important repeated word. Paul didn't simply say that Epaphroditus was a brother, worker, soldier, messenger, and minister. Paul instead describes him as a *fellow* worker and a *fellow* soldier. Epaphroditus wasn't just a behind-the-scenes guy; he was working alongside Paul.

What would that look like for us? How can we be women who work alongside those we believe in? When we join, our vital work will expand and make a mark on the world around us.

Be a woman of bold influence because you believe in a generous God. Be a woman who loves others who don't necessarily look like you, speak like you, vote like you, live like you. Be a woman who gives so much it sometimes hurts, stepping outside your comfort zone and leaning on Christ's strength. Be the kind of woman who wears different hats, not because you're caught up in the pursuit of busy but because you want to make your one life count for the glory of God.

Talk to the Lord about all the different hats you wear. Which ones do you sense Him asking you to pick up, and which should you set aside?

Amen.

WEEK 4 • *Day 4*

 READ PHILIPPIANS 2:25-30

One of my Instagram friends shared this week that her daughter had a short fall and suffered a fluke traumatic brain injury. The news sounded grim and scary. Her daughter was hooked up to all sorts of tubes and wires. Halfway through my friend's post, though, she offered a powerful reminder:

+ + But God + +

Today as I sat down to dive into this Scripture again with you, these two words leaped from the pages of my Bible: *But God.* God can do all things, big and small—and He is the Great Healer (Exodus 15:26). I'm praying He shows mercy to my sweet friend's daughter just as he did to Epaphroditus:

> Indeed he was ill, near to death. *But God* had mercy on
> him, and not only on him but on me also, lest I should have
> sorrow upon sorrow.
> PHILIPPIANS 2:27, EMPHASIS MINE

Epaphroditus had traveled to Rome, bearing a gift from the Philippian church (we learn this in Philippians 4:18), and became ill somewhere along the way. How difficult that had to have been for Paul, who loved this man as a brother!

I've struggled with migraines for over fifteen years and have a whole slew of other health issues. When I'm sick, I'm often really, *really* sick. When I get a migraine, it feels like my head is going to explode. It's hard to think straight, let alone worry about what's going on with the people around me.

When our oldest son, Abreham, came home to us at nearly fourteen years old, he had already experienced massive loss. Sadly, Ethiopia doesn't have the quality of medical care we do here in the States, and illness often leads to death, especially in the tiny, remote village where Abreham was born. A few short weeks after he joined our family, I was struck with another migraine—my first since he'd come home—and couldn't get out of bed. Ben found Abreham weeping quietly on the stairs. Through many attempts to bridge the massive language gap and understand what was wrong, Ben realized Abreham thought I was dying. Our newest son thought he was going to lose another mom. My heart broke for his anguish, and I forced myself to get up and pretend I was okay.

I cared more about Abreham's suffering than my own. And we see something similar from Epaphroditus in these verses: Even in his illness, he was distressed about the Philippian church's worry (Philippians 2:26).

Yesterday we learned of all the ways Epaphroditus helped Paul once he regained his health. And yet Paul was willing—in fact Paul said he was *eager*—to send Epaphroditus back home to Philippi (Philippians 2:28).

1. If Epaphroditus had been such an incredible help and blessing to Paul, why would Paul be eager to send back his brother and fellow soldier?

God spared Epaphroditus for the sake of Paul, so Paul may have felt he could (or should) spare him for the sake of the Philippians. In other words, Paul knew it wasn't all about him.

Let's go back to the text itself as we dig in deeper.

2. Look back to Philippians 2:27 and circle the words *sorrow upon sorrow*. What do you think Paul is trying to express? (Hint: Feel free to share your personal theories here. You're also welcome to head to the BLB and look up the words in the *Interlinear* or even head to a commentary to assist in your answer.)

_____

_____

_____

Paul says that God showed mercy to him. Paul has gone through many sorrows, and he fully believes that God so graciously healed his fellow soldier and minister in part to protect him from more sorrow. Consider what we know about Paul's sorrow just from the book of Philippians:

a. He is imprisoned (1:7).
b. Fellow believers are preaching with "envy and rivalry," taking advantage of the fact that Paul's in jail (1:15).
c. He endures mental and spiritual struggle from not knowing whether he will be martyred or set free (1:19-21).
d. Paul emotionally and physically suffers for the sake of Christ, engaging in conflict, or *agōn* (ἀγών, pronounced *ah-gohn*) (1:29-30).
e. Paul struggles knowing that other believers are doing things with conceit and their own interests above that of Christ's (2:3).

This list is far from exhaustive, but you get the point. Paul's life is hard, and he's seriously struggling in a myriad of ways. Everything he faced should have bowled him over, right? Paul was certainly handed a lot more than any human can carry.

3. We've all heard the saying *God won't give you more than you can handle.* But is that idea, in fact, biblical? Why or why not?

I think people mean well when they declare, "God won't give you more than you can handle," but this is massively poor theology. And you won't find this idea anywhere in Scripture. In fact, we consistently see the opposite: God often allows us to face more than we can handle, but He is sufficient in the midst of it. He wants to carry all of the things we can't handle.

So where do we even get the idea that God won't give us more than we can handle? Let's check out something from Paul's letter to the Corinthian church:

> No temptation has overtaken you that is not common to man. God is faithful, and he will not let you be tempted beyond your ability, but with the temptation he will also provide the way of escape, that you may be able to endure it.
> 1 CORINTHIANS 10:13

When we look at this verse in isolation, we miss the full picture of what God is trying to communicate to us through His Word. We cannot simply pull a singular verse from the Bible and make it say what we want it to say. So, let's flip over to 1 Corinthians 10 to find out what's going on.

4. What have translators titled that chapter in your version of the Bible?

Most versions of the Bible indicate that this chapter is about idolatry. Paul reminds the Corinthians about Moses and the Israelites who were brought out of slavery in Egypt—how all that they ate and drank was provided by God Himself. As the Israelites wandered the wilderness, God gave them everything they needed day by day. Check out how *The Message* translation describes it:

> But just experiencing God's wonder and grace didn't seem
> to mean much—most of them were defeated by temptation
> during the hard times in the desert, and God was not pleased.
>   The same thing could happen to us. We must be on
> guard so that we never get caught up in wanting our own
> way as they did.
> 1 CORINTHIANS 10:5-6, MSG

Paul's main point in this passage is that the Israelites are an example of what *not* to do. We are just as capable of messing up as they were, so we need to learn from their example!

> These are all warning markers—DANGER!—in our history
> books, written down so that we don't repeat their mistakes. Our
> positions in the story are parallel—they at the beginning, we
> at the end—and we are just as capable of messing it up as they
> were. Don't be so naive and self-confident. You're not exempt.
> You could fall flat on your face as easily as anyone else. Forget
> about self-confidence; it's useless. Cultivate God-confidence.
> 1 CORINTHIANS 10:11-12, MSG

5. Read 1 Corinthians 10:13 in *The Message*, then head back to the ESV to study the literal text. What does this full passage indicate about God giving us more than we can handle?

This verse is very specific about what God promises: not that He will keep us from *anything* more than we can bear, but rather that He will not allow more *temptation* than we can bear. But what does this word *temptation* really mean?

6. Check out this phrase in the *Interlinear*: *you to be tempted* (*peirazō*; πειράζω, pronounced *pay-rad-zo*)

I found this part of the definition particularly helpful: "By impious or wicked conduct to test God's justice and patience, and to challenge him, as it were to give proof of his perfections." Or, as another part of the definition puts it, temptation means "to try or test one's faith, virtue, character, by enticement to sin."[13]

This is kind of a mic-drop moment, right? This is essentially what Paul is saying: Whatever you're being enticed to do, you're not the first who has struggled with it. God is faithful, and clinging to Him is the way out for anything that's testing your faith, virtue, or character in sin. The Lord will not abandon you in your sin or in your temptation. He will provide a way for you to endure.

This doesn't say anything about sorrow or difficulties or suffering, does it? Our promise from God is that in Him, we will be able to resist temptation.

7. How has understanding this passage in more depth changed the way you see the concept of God not giving you more than you can handle? What do you think this means in the context of Paul's *sorrow upon sorrow* in Philippians 2:27 (ESV)?

Look back to Philippians 2:28 and notice the word *therefore* (I'm in the ESV). As we've learned, that word connects back to what preceded it: in this case, the idea in Philippians 2:27 that God had mercy on Epaphroditus and healed him for the benefit of Paul and the gospel. God had given Paul far more than he could handle already—and through relying on God's strength in his weakness (2 Corinthians 12:9-11) Paul had continued in his work for the gospel in the midst of it. God's healing of Epaphroditus was pure mercy, intervention to protect Paul from this particular sorrow in the midst of everything else.

Of course, as much as I'd like to say we won't face struggles in our lives, I know that's not true . . . and so do you. We live in a fallen world full of imperfect people—and Jesus Himself told us, "In this world you will have trouble" (John 16:33, NIV). Following God in a world broken by sin means that we will face pain and hardship and death itself. Sometimes, God's mercy steps between us and that pain, and that is a gift. But the greater gift is what Jesus promised immediately after telling us we will have trouble: "But take heart! I have overcome the world." Because we live in Him who has overcome the world, we will be carried through whatever trouble we face.

Talk to God about a hard situation you are walking through. Pray that He will give you the strength to endure today and each day as you cling to Him tighter through your hard season.

Amen.

WEEK 4 • *Day 5*

 READ PHILIPPIANS 2:25-30

My dear friend Karissa calls herself a Super Survivor. She survived the shooting at Columbine High School as a freshman and becoming a war widow shortly after saying "I do." She has also survived stage 4 cancer three times and is currently battling it again. From a human perspective, we might think she should do what Job's wife suggested in the face of unending pain: "curse God and die" (Job 2:9). But you know what? She doesn't. And what's more, she's one of the most light-filled, joyful women I know.

When pain slams into our lives, we can find it so easy to be angry at God. After all, if He really is in control of all things, why didn't He just prevent the pain? Couldn't He have saved our spouse from that accident? Or kept our child from addiction? Or intervened before that relationship fell apart?

The problem of pain and suffering is one that we all have to wrestle with. It's a complex and difficult reality that ultimately comes down to our faith and trust in the God we follow. Sometimes the things that wound us are a result of a broken and sinful world that God is working to make new. Sometimes it's the result of our sin, or the ways someone else has sinned against us. And sometimes, in ways we can't even comprehend, God uses the thing that causes us pain for the good of others.

If we try to run out of our hard season and into an easy one too fast, we may miss what God wants to do in the midst of it. God doesn't waste experiences, and He certainly doesn't waste time.

> *If Jesus gives us a task or assigns us to a*
> *difficult season, every ounce of our experience*
> *is meant for our instruction and completion*
> *if only we'll let Him finish the work. I fear,*
> *however, that we are so attention-deficit*
> *that we settle for bearable when beauty*
> *is just around the corner.*[14]
>
> BETH MOORE

1. What do you believe about God's work in our pain? Be honest—God can handle it.

Today in Philippians, we get to see Paul holding the tension of his honest feelings of sorrow—and the sorrow he would have felt had his dear friend died—and his recognition that his pain and needs came second to God's greater work. As I read his words in Philippians 2:28, I find myself reminded of what he said earlier in the chapter:

> [3] Do nothing from selfish ambition or conceit, but in humility count others more significant than yourselves. [4] Let each of you look not only to his own interests, but also to the interests of others.
>
> PHILIPPIANS 2:3-4

2. How does Philippians 2:3-4 connect to Paul's perspective on Epaphroditus and the Philippian church?

_____

_____

_____

In His mercy, God kept Paul from the added sorrow of losing his dear friend, and in response, Paul lives out his own words from Philippians 2:3-4 (and 2:21-22—placing others above himself). Epaphroditus was a significant person in the work of the gospel and in Paul's life, particularly during his imprisonment, yet Paul quickly turns to how God can use his friend for the sake of the gospel and the Philippian church.

3. What does Paul say will be the result if his dear friend is sent back to Philippi (Philippians 2:28)?

_____

_____

_____

Why would Epaphroditus being in Philippi make Paul less anxious? Wouldn't _not_ sending him home be better for Paul? Epaphroditus has been such an immense help to Paul in his imprisonment!

But Paul has spent this whole letter telling the Philippians what it looks like to live a life that really matters. We see the heart of it in Philippians 2:3-8.

4. Flip back to that passage, and rephrase the essence of the passage:

_____

_____

_____

Paul knows that he cannot just tell the Philippians what makes up a life that really matters—he has to live it himself. That means valuing others above himself, looking to the interests of others, choosing to humble himself in obedience to the call of God. *Do what I say, not as I do* doesn't work in any part of life—especially in living out the way of Jesus.

5. Where in your life do you struggle to match up your words with your actions? How could you align those things in pursuit of the life that really matters?

I hate goodbyes. One of my favorite people in the world, who lives kitty-corner from me, just put their house up for sale. I'm trying to be excited for their next adventure . . . but I'm feeling myself pushing back, disconnecting, guarding my heart. Goodbyes are painful, and I've done too many of them.

I could learn a thing or two from Paul, though. As he faces saying goodbye to a dear friend, his response isn't grief or detachment or fear. Instead, he looks to the bigger picture, God's larger purpose, the fact that the thing that may pain him will ultimately be for the good of so many others.

None of us wants to go through pain. None of us wants to say goodbye to the people we love. But let's take our hearts to God, knowing that He is crafting something beautiful in spite of the ache.

Take some time to pray for those you've had to say goodbye to, those who have pursued God's calling on their lives. Maybe they've moved on from where you work, from your community or your city, or even from your country. Perhaps they've simply moved into a new season of life. Ask God to settle your heart in the knowledge that He is working great things, even in our goodbyes.

Amen.

WEEK 4 • *Notes*

Share your biggest takeaways from this week:

Watch and Learn

Philippians 3:1–4:1

WEEK 5 • *Day 1*

 READ PHILIPPIANS 3:1-3

Since he was eight or nine, our son Laith has wanted to come into "big church" with us rather than going to Sunday school like his siblings. He's a fan of learning and says he absorbs more from our pastor's sermon than from class with the other kids. But during the summer, he's pretty eager for church to be over. You see, in the summer, our church does Sunday night church, and we celebrate community after each service with food, games, and new and old friends. Every service, I watch Laith perk up when our pastor uses words like *finally*, a signal that the sermon is wrapping up. *Finally* means he's almost allowed to beeline outside to eat and play.

If Laith had been part of the Philippian church, listening to this letter being read, I think he would have been frustrated at Paul's use of *finally* here. We're in chapter 3 . . . out of four. Paul says *finally* (Philippians 3:1) and then simply continues!

But there's another strange shift in the beginning of this chapter. After speaking warmly to the church, urging unity and affirming humility and celebrating his friends, Paul suddenly switches his tone. In Philippians 3:2—talking in harsh terms about dogs, evildoers, and those who mutilate the flesh—he sounds a bit disgruntled, right? Where did this come from?

Some commentators believe that while writing this part of the letter, Paul received news of people creating drama and confusion within the church at Philippi. But this is where it's important for us to look at the broader context in Scripture, because I'm not quite sure that explanation holds up.

1. Paul has been writing about Timothy and Epaphroditus, but what was he talking about before that?

Philippians 2 is all about Christ's example of humility and being a light in the world. Paul explains that joy isn't an individual pursuit but rather something that should be shared in unity with the body of Christ, and then he pauses to use Timothy and Epaphroditus as examples of what this joy in community looks like. Now, here in Philippians 3, he's resuming his joy theme.

That brings us back to this word *finally*. In English, this is the word we'd use to wrap things up—we'd think that Paul was about to end the letter, roll it up, seal it with wax, and send it off with Epaphroditus. Yet he's got much more to say! So maybe *finally* doesn't mean what we think it means. Let's look at the Greek for *Finally my brothers* (*loipos ego adelphos*; λοιπός ἐγώ ἀδελφός).

Many of our Bibles translate *loipos* (λοιπός, pronounced *loi-pas*) as *finally*, but if we look at the *Thayer's Greek Lexicon*, we see *loipos* (λοιπός) defined in ways that make much more sense for our context: "henceforth," "besides, moreover."[1]

2. Use one of these words to fill in the beginning of verse 1:

_____ my brothers,

rejoice in the Lord.

PHILIPPIANS 3:1

This word *loipos* acts as a bridge between what Paul has been teaching (about joy and living as a light) and what he is about to teach (rejoicing in the Lord). This link is important, because Paul is about to make that swerve we talked about: into the greatest threat against true joy in Christ.

3. What does he call these threats to joy?

Do you know what these descriptions signify? Opponents of the gospel. But what exactly does he mean by each of these phrases?

When Paul talks about looking out for dogs, he doesn't mean being afraid of our cuddly pet friends and loving companions. At the time, in Paul's culture, dogs represented everything that was repugnant and depraved. Many Jews called Gentiles "dogs," and Paul would have done the same in his pharisaical years. But that's not what he's doing now. (Remember, he has Gentile brothers who are partners in the gospel!)

4. Whom is Paul referring to?

When I look at the notes in my *ESV Study Bible,* I find the answer: "With biting irony, Paul says that the Judaizers, not the Gentiles, deserve that label."[2] Paul doesn't stop there—he also calls Judaizers, those who focus on human good works through the law, "evildoers" and "those who mutilate the flesh."

What Paul means here by *mutilate the flesh* is circumcision. Christianity was originally seen as a sect of Judaism, and for Jews in the early church (and Jews observing the early church), the big question was, "Are these Gentiles in this offshoot of Judaism going to live according to the law?" Paul says, "Absolutely not." In the Jewish faith, circumcision was a sign of dedication to God, so the idea of people following God and *not* being circumcised would have infuriated and horrified especially pious Jews.[3]

5. Why do you think Paul is against Gentile Christ followers having to live according to Jewish law?

_____

_____

_____

The Jewish faith had become focused on trying to follow all the rules in order to be right with God. But Jesus' life, death, and resurrection showed that *Jesus* was the only way people could be right with God. Any other way—anything that we add on top of following Jesus—is not the gospel.

In fact, this was why Paul wrote his letter to the Galatian church. After Paul planted the church and helped this community of new believers grow, it became saturated with distorted practices in a remarkably short time. The people had abandoned the true gospel and instead started following a group of false teachers—the Judaizers. The Judaizers both bad-mouthed Paul and told the Gentile believers that they must be circumcised in order to truly be followers of Jesus. The Judaizers in Galatia claimed to follow Jesus, but they didn't understand that Jesus came for *all* people. Non-Jews didn't need to become Jewish to follow Him.

We see it again in Philippians: Paul gets super riled up when anyone spreads a false gospel. He understands that when we're swept up in misinformation and mistruth, we cannot possibly have a right relationship with Christ—nor can we have unity within believers.

6. What false gospels ("being a Christian means following Jesus plus . . .") do you see in our world today?

_____

_____

_____

_____

I really want you to think hard on this one. If you don't know how to answer it, stop to pray and ponder awhile. People have been adding things to the Good News of Jesus since the time of the early church, and it's no different today. Paul shows us here that it's vital we pay attention to what's false and remember what's true.

7. What will you do to stop false gospel? How can you elevate the essential truth of the Good News in your everyday life?

Part of living for what really matters is understanding the truth of the gospel and being willing to call out mistruth within culture—or even within the Christian community. The gospel transforms lives, but adding to the gospel creates barriers to really knowing and following Jesus. Are we willing to be like Paul and stand up for the true gospel in the face of opposition?

Thank God for the gift of wisdom and discernment, and ask Him to continue developing it in you so you can keep your steps in line with Him and point others—in love—toward the right way too.

Amen.

WEEK 5 • *Day 2*

 READ PHILIPPIANS 3:4-8

What makes a good Christian? If you were to list the markers of someone who's doing this following-Jesus thing right, what would you say?

Paul shares his "pedigree" with us in today's passage, and it's pretty impressive, right? Each of us, no matter if we started following Jesus when we were a child or last week, can be tempted to build up a list like this as the "proof" of our dedication to Him. Here's my list of credentials—let's see if you think it shows I love Jesus and am living for Him:

- I'm from a Christian family. My mom was a leader in Bible Study Fellowship, my dad led men's groups and mentored many young professionals, and together they led the "young marrieds" Sunday school class at our church for over a decade.

- I "asked Jesus into my heart" at age five.

- I went to Christian elementary, middle, and high schools.

- My family lived in Guatemala for a few years—partly for business and partly for ministry.

- The first concert I went to featured Michael W. Smith.

- I played the handbells in church.

- I purchased numerous copies of *Wild at Heart* and *Captivating* when they came out, so I could give them to all my friends.

- I went to a Christian university.

- I wore a purity ring throughout high school and college.

- I went to Bible school in England and studied ancient Greek.

Because of all this, I must be super close in my walk with God, right? I mean, isn't this list what it's all about?

Well . . . no.

God doesn't look at our pedigree or the list of things we've done "right"—He looks at our hearts and how we live. The list doesn't matter much. My husband's list is pretty much the opposite of my shiny, happy, Jesus-y one: Abuse. Homelessness. Pain. But he loves Jesus and is deeply committed to following Him, and that's the only thing that matters to God.

Why does Paul list his credentials here? All things considered, they were impeccable.

1. What does Paul say in verse 4?

What Paul is saying here is, "If there were a competition on being the Most Awesome Jew, I'd win first prize." But let's dig into the details of what he's saying, using the following passage. (Keep your study Bible handy—referencing multiple translations can enhance our understanding of a passage!)

2. In the text below, please number all seven aspects Paul includes as his "pedigree."

> ³ We are the circumcision, who worship by the Spirit of God and glory in Christ Jesus and put no confidence in the flesh—⁴ though I myself have reason for confidence in the flesh also. If anyone else thinks he has reason for confidence in the flesh, I have more: ⁵ circumcised on the eighth day, of the people of Israel, of the tribe of Benjamin, a Hebrew of Hebrews; as to the law, a Pharisee; ⁶ as to zeal, a persecutor of the church; as to righteousness under the law, blameless. ⁷ But whatever gain I had, I counted as loss for the sake of Christ. ⁸ Indeed, I count everything as loss because of the surpassing worth of knowing Christ Jesus my Lord. For his sake I have suffered the loss of all things and count them as rubbish, in order that I may gain Christ ⁹ and be found in him, not having a righteousness of my own that comes from the law, but that which comes through faith in Christ, the righteousness from God that depends on faith.
>
> PHILIPPIANS 3:3-9

 History Lesson

Paul's credentials were hugely important in the Jewish culture he grew up in. Here's what each piece would have meant:

- *circumcised on the eighth day*—as every good Jewish boy was, according to Old Testament law (Leviticus 12:3)
- *of the people of Israel*—part of God's elect and chosen people
- *of the tribe of Benjamin*—the smallest of all twelve tribes held a special place in the hearts of many because Benjamin was the youngest son of Jacob; King Saul (the first king of Israel) was also a Benjaminite (1 Samuel 9:21)

- *a Hebrew of Hebrews*—Paul descended from a long line of Jewish ancestors. Some believe he calls himself this because he likely spoke Aramaic, the national language of Jews in the day.
- *a Pharisee*—the strictest religious sect
- *zealous*—he was a bit of a fanatic: earnest, dedicated, and passionate about the law
- *a persecutor of the church*—when Paul persecuted the Christians, he likely thought of himself as protecting his religion, following in the footsteps of Phinehas (Numbers 25:11) and Elijah (1 Kings 19:10, 14).
- *blameless*—Paul was a major rule follower . . . or, in this case, law follower; over time, the Pharisees added many extra laws to God's original commandments.[4]

The Jews would have seen everything Paul listed as important and prestigious. But Paul isn't listing his credentials to show off. No—he has a different purpose.

3. What does Paul say he's doing to his pedigree or credentials? Why?

_____

_____

_____

_____

4. If being a Christian isn't about our pedigree or what we've done, what *is* the mark of a true believer in Jesus?

_____

_____

_____

_____

The *real* believers are the ones the Spirit of God leads to
work away at this ministry, filling the air with Christ's praise
as we do it.

PHILIPPIANS 3:3, MSG

My ESV translates this verse as "For we are the circumcision." But
if Paul is saying we don't need to be circumcised, why is he calling
us *the circumcision*?

5. Why do you think Paul is using this term?

Circumcision was a physical sign that set the Israelites apart from
the world around them, identifying them as God's chosen people. But
under the new covenant, anyone who believes Jesus is the Messiah
becomes God's chosen people. Because we are the men and women
of God, Paul is saying *we are* the circumcision. Our very lives identify
us as chosen by God. Because of Jesus, this term has a new meaning
(see Romans 2:28-29). Circumcision is no longer physical but is now
spiritual.

In Philippians 3:5-6, Paul tells the Philippian church (and us)
about who he used to be. He was the young, rising star in the Pharisaic
community—in part because of his dedication and wisdom, but also
because of how intensely he persecuted the followers of Jesus. But when
he met Jesus on the road to Damascus (Acts 9), everything changed.
He realized that all he once held dear and all that he once thought
important was rubbish—because nothing compared to knowing Jesus.

Once we start following Jesus, once we really understand what
it means to love and be loved by Him, the things we once thought
were important or fun can suddenly seem uninteresting. Or perhaps

setting those things aside is still a struggle, but we begin to comprehend their negative impact.

6. What things have you set aside or felt prompted to change in the course of your walk with Jesus?

_____

_____

_____

7. What have you gained as you've followed Jesus?

_____

_____

_____

You, my sweet sister, are a world changer because you have chosen to follow Jesus. Those losses? They're not actually losses. A loss is a deficit, and the One who loves you has given you only abundance and sufficiency. In Jesus, you've gained more than you can ever imagine.

Talk to the Lord about how you might be tempted to step into checklist-Christianity mode. Ask Him to remind you that God doesn't love us because of all the things we do for Him—He loves us because He is love and He has saved us.

_____

_____

_____

_____

_____

Amen.

WEEK 5 • *Day 3*

 READ PHILIPPIANS 3:9-11

I am a rule follower to the core. As a kid, I'd get in trouble simply because I *looked* so guilty! Even the idea of doing something wrong— or someone else thinking I'd done something wrong—made me break out in a sweat and a big ol' nervous smile.

I've rarely colored outside the lines, rarely done things I knew I wasn't supposed to. I recently had to go to court for leaving our garbage cans visible too long. No, I'm not kidding. I got the date wrong and missed my first court appointment, so I got a letter saying if I didn't appear this next time, there'd be a warrant out for my arrest. I told my kids, *this is why you follow the rules!*

People seeing me as a goody-goody rule follower was sometimes annoying, so when I was younger I'd occasionally try to do something I considered really bad to seem more relatable. (Once, in high school, I decided to use a minor curse word for a day . . . and immediately felt like I should wash my own mouth out with soap.)

Just following the rules doesn't get you anywhere with God. My husband has quite a non-rule-follower story, and when he met Jesus, our heavenly Father helped him out of the muck and mire of his past, present, and likely his future—just as He did for me. No matter where we've come from or what we've done, we all find ourselves in need of God's extravagant grace.

That's what Paul is talking about today in Philippians. In Philippians 3:8-9, he says,

> ⁸ Indeed, I count everything as loss because of the surpassing worth of knowing Christ Jesus my Lord. For his sake I have suffered the loss of all things and count them as rubbish, in order that I may gain Christ ⁹ and be found in him, not having a righteousness of my own that comes from the law, but that which comes through faith in Christ, the righteousness from God that depends on faith.
>
> PHILIPPIANS 3:8-9

As a zealous Pharisee, Paul had been addicted to trying to follow all the Jewish laws because he felt he was right. Being right and perfect—or at least feeling like he was better at it than everyone else—gave him his feeling of worth.

But this is what Paul realized—and this is important:

We will never be good enough for God.

I know we don't like hearing that. Except it's not even like when your boyfriend's sister comes up to you and says, "You'll never be good enough for him," because we literally *won't* ever be good enough for Him! God is the Creator of the universe, the Creator of you and me, and is good and holy and perfect in a way we can't even fathom. But that's what's so incredible about grace and mercy: God meets us where we are through the sacrifice of Jesus Christ.

Let's dive into Philippians 3:9 in the BLB to learn more about what Paul means by "righteousness."

1. Looking through the *Interlinear* for this passage, what does the word *righteousness* (*dikaiosynē*; δικαιοσύνη, pronounced *di-kai-o-soo-nay*) mean?

2. If you were to write in those phrases and descriptions of *dikaiosynē* (δικαιοσύνη), how would you use it to rewrite verse 9?

> . . . in order that I may gain Christ and be found in him, not having a _____ of my own that comes from the law, but that which comes through faith in Christ, the _____ from God that depends on faith.

3. What is the difference between achieving righteousness on our own and understanding that righteousness comes only through faith in Christ? How can you consciously set aside your elevation of the things you think make you "right" with God and rest in the faith that He has already made you right?

Pursuing self-righteousness means a life of striving and failing—a life of trying to live apart from God. Living a life of God-focused righteousness means living in relationship with Him because He has made us right. We are enough because He has made us enough.

Last night I was texting back and forth with a sweet friend who is on the run from her abusive husband. This past fall, when she and I were at a retreat, her aunt and uncle sneaked her out. She's been in hiding for the past few months. She's about to face her husband in court for the first time, and as you can imagine, she is so stressed out about seeing him again. Over the years of abuse, she's begun to believe the lies this man has spouted over her. His words and his actions spoke death into her sense of self.

Abuse makes us believe that we will never be good enough, that we must constantly strive for worthiness, that our efforts can somehow change the darkness in the other person. And whether we've experienced abuse or not, our hustling for worthiness[5] can affect our relationship with God, as well. For my friend, the idea of never being good enough for God hurts because she doesn't feel good enough for anyone right now.

We must hold on to this important truth: self-righteousness, striving, and success are not what God is looking for. Neither is feeling shame and dwelling on the idea that we're not good enough for His love. His love is not dependent on us being good enough—and that's incredible news, because not one of us is. God's love means that He welcomes you as you are and will never leave you the way He found you. You are worthy because He calls you worthy, and you become more like Him because He makes you more like Him.

Talk to God about the truth that you can come to Him just as you are. Ask for Him to help you rest in any places where you are striving for worthiness. He welcomes you whether you feel dirty and beaten down or buttoned-up and shiny.

Amen.

WEEK 5 ● *Day 4*

 READ PHILIPPIANS 3:12-16

Maybe it's just me, but the fact that Paul feels like a work in progress is pretty comforting. This incredible man of God, who had a profound influence on the early church, was human just like me. And in his humanness, he shows us how to pursue a life of trusting the Lord rather than trusting in our own ability to be perfect. Because we all have the tendency and face the temptation to take control of our life's helm ourselves.

My rule-following ways became a desire for perfectionism. After all, if I could follow all the rules just so, I could control myself and all the things around me, too—right? I've also been known to look for my worth in perfectionism. Amanda Jenkins wrote poignantly about this impulse in her book *Confessions of a Raging Perfectionist*:

> To be thought of as the bravest or the wisest. To be
> recognized for having the cleanest house and the best-
> behaved kids (which would make me the best mom, right?).
> I want my husband to think I'm the sexiest, my mom to
> think I'm the kindest, and my friends to think I'm the
> funniest.[6]

That list we talked about yesterday? I run into problems when I attach significance to it—that "if I lose five pounds and spend twenty minutes reading my Bible, I'll be a better, more spiritual, more loving, more *lovable* person. When I fail to live up to my own expectations, I feel inadequate . . . unworthy of the approval I seek."[7]

For Christian women, that's a tragic irony—
tragic because, like everyone else, we spend
most of our time working toward unattainable
goals; ironic because Christ died to free us
from the notion that we must earn our worth.[8]

AMANDA JENKINS

1. Does perfectionism have a hold over your life? Where do you struggle with the need to be perfect to gain approval?

What if, instead of pursuing perfection, we pursued the One who is perfect? When we want to be like Christ, we're not struggling for the kind of perfection that means we look perfect—and so do our kids and house. God isn't interested in us simply looking the part. He's interested in restoring us so we can live in increasing intimacy with Him.

2. What do you think is the difference between striving through perfectionism and striving toward Someone who is perfect?

What I've learned about striving toward perfection and living a life of rule-following is that I'm doing things *for* God rather than being *with* God. I don't need to prove to God that I'm worthy of love because I'm a perfect rule follower. I couldn't, even if I tried. He loves me just because I'm His daughter and because it's in His very nature to love.

3. Head to Philippians 3:12 in the BLB and look at the word *perfect* in the *Interlinear*. How would you rewrite the first part of Philippians 3:12, using the words and phrases from the *Interlinear* section or even *Thayer's Greek Lexicon*?

Here's what I got: *I'm not saying that I have already accomplished this goal of being found complete and raised to the state of heavenly blessedness through perfection, but I press on toward it.* Your rewording is probably similar to mine, but I'm not quite seeing how this helps me break free of perfectionism. Do you? Let's see what else the Bible tells us about being perfect—maybe that will clarify things. Check out Matthew 5:48:

You therefore must be perfect, as your heavenly Father is perfect.

4. Wait a second. We're supposed to be perfect, as it says in Matthew 5 . . . but we have no way to achieve perfection because only God is perfect? What do you think this means?

God, who is perfect, requires perfection from us because only the perfect can be in His presence. We become perfect not through anything we do, but rather because of God's great exchange: As we believe in and accept Jesus' sacrificial death on the cross, He exchanges our imperfection for His perfection. Then we, as new creations, receive the Holy Spirit, who dwells inside us, cultivating our lives so that we can become more like Jesus.[9]

5. In Philippians 3:13, Paul says that he hasn't yet arrived at his goal. How is he actively pursuing it?

Sometimes we think we're unchangeable, that we're stuck in who we are and how we live. But even though we may feel enmeshed and bogged down, it's because we've conditioned ourselves to believe we can't come untangled. That's a lie! If we seek God's face and pray with a humble heart, He can change us. What we thought were immovable aspects in our character will shift to show His glory instead of seek our own. There are always second chances with God.

In Philippians 3:14, Paul proclaims he is actively pursuing the heart of God for a specific prize: "the upward call of God in Christ Jesus."

6. How do Paul's words here in Philippians 3:14 connect to what he says in 1 Corinthians 9:24?

This verse in 1 Corinthians always makes me think of my oldest son, Abreham. Several of my kids are runners, but so far, Abreham's four-minute-twenty-second mile makes him the fastest. One thing Abreham's high-school coach always told him was, "Don't look back—it slows you down!" So when Paul shares in Philippians 3:13 that he's not looking back, but forward, I'm reminded that the words of Abreham's coach are true in life as well. If we're focused on where we came from and how we measure up to others, how are we going to focus on where we're going and pursue it well?

There's another piece to this whole perfection conversation that we find in Philippians 3:15, and it connects to what Paul is saying about the race in a way that should expand our understanding far beyond ourselves. Depending on what translation you're studying from, you may not even know these words are present in verse 15, but this verse literally says,

> [15] Let us therefore, as many as are perfect, have this attitude; and if in anything you have a different attitude, God will reveal that also to you; [16] however, let us keep living by that same standard to which we have attained.
>
> PHILIPPIANS 3:15-16, NASB

So he's saying the word *us* next to the phrase *as many as are perfect*? I thought perfection was unattainable! But now he's telling us that he and we and others are part of a community of perfect people? Let's dig into what he means by *perfect* here. It makes sense; I promise.

7. Grab your phone and head to the BLB again. What do you learn about this phrase *be perfect* (*teleios*; τέλειος, pronounced *teh-lay-os*)? (Hint: Look in *Thayer's Greek Lexicon*.)

Did you find the part where it says that *teleios* means someone
who is "full-grown" and "mature"?[10] This word means that something
has grown into beautiful maturity.

In Philippians 3:15, Paul isn't saying that he's perfect or that anyone else is either. Instead, we can grow into maturity in Christ—
together. Every piece of wisdom we learn, every choice we make to
depend on God, every move we make to live like Christ (Matthew 5),
leads us toward maturity and God's perfecting work. Paul knows some
of us haven't reached that place of maturity (Philippians 3:15-16).
But when we choose to be in God's Word and intentionally deepen
our roots, we are growing. We are always moving toward the One
who is perfect.

Consider the places in your life where you struggle with perfectionism, and place them at the feet of Jesus. Take some time
in silence today—while driving in your car, while sweeping or
doing dishes, or any time you would typically turn on music
or the television—to hear how He wants to make you perfect
according to His will, not your efforts. Meet the Lord in the
silence. What is He whispering over you?

Amen.

WEEK 5 • *Day 5*

 READ PHILIPPIANS 3:17–4:1

All this talk of running a race and pressing on can feel overwhelming when we're worn down, right? I'm emotionally exhausted and mega-stressed today. I feel like life is a bit much right now. But while Paul is still talking about pursuing the life that matters, his words in our passage today are like cool, thirst-quenching water to my parched and weary soul, a reminder that this pressing on and race running does not ultimately depend on me:

> 17-19 Stick with me, friends. Keep track of those you see running this same course, headed for this same goal. There are many out there taking other paths, choosing other goals, and trying to get you to go along with them. I've warned you of them many times; sadly, I'm having to do it again. All they want is easy street. They hate Christ's Cross. But easy street is a dead-end street. Those who live there make their bellies their gods; belches are their praise; all they can think of is their appetites.
>
> 20-21 But there's far more to life for us. We're citizens of high heaven! We're waiting the arrival of the Savior, the Master, Jesus Christ, who will transform our earthy bodies into glorious bodies like his own. He'll make us beautiful and whole with the same powerful skill by which he is putting everything as it should be, under and around him.
>
> PHILIPPIANS 3:17-21, MSG

Paul is covering a lot of ground in these short verses, but do you see those encouraging words at the end? In the midst of our race, in the midst of all the competing goals and voices, we await the transformation and wholeness that Jesus offers.

This is the second time within the span of a few verses that Paul has asked us to live according to his example. From Paul's mini-testimony in Philippians 3:4-13 to verse 14 calling us to *press on*, Paul has set a standard (set first by Jesus Himself) that he encourages us all to follow. Suddenly, however, here in verses 17-18, his tone shifts to a stiff and sobering warning.

1. What three things in verse 19 does Paul warn the Philippian church (and us) to watch out for from these "enemies of the cross of Christ"?

The idea of someone hating or simply not caring about God (both of which mean an absence of relationship with Him) grips Paul's heart to the point of tears (Philippians 3:18). This word *tears* (*klaiō*; κλαίω, pronounced *klai-oh*) means more literally "to mourn, weep, lament: weeping as the sign of pain and grief," "weep[ing] of those who mourn for the dead."[11]

There is a deeper passion in this ancient Greek word than we find in English, isn't there? The idea of someone being against God, walking in enmity against Him, deeply affects Paul and grieves him to his very core.

Loving Jesus and following Him is a conscious choice; tragically, it's a choice many people do not make. Our friends, our family members, our coworkers, neighbors, and acquaintances may be "taking other paths, choosing other goals" (Philippians 3:18, MSG) than the life that really matters. And that reality should devastate us as deeply as it does Paul.

In many places throughout this letter to the Philippians, Paul has talked about how to live a life that really matters and has called for unity and imitation. Here in 3:19, however, Paul gives us a negative example, contrasting everything he's been outlining with the kind of life we should reject because it leads to destruction.

This word *destruction* (*apōleia*; ἀπώλεια, pronounced *ah-poh-lay-ah*) is interesting. When we look it up in the BLB, we see it does indeed mean "ruin, utter destruction, and that which consists of eternal misery in hell." But *apōleia* also means something else. This word is used in various places within the New Testament when referring to waste. Here's an example of our same word *apōleia* in Matthew 26, when a woman pours expensive ointment over Jesus' head as a sacrifice of love to Him:

> And when the disciples saw it, they were indignant, saying, "Why this waste?"
>
> MATTHEW 26:8

Waste is destruction, and the ultimate form of destruction is a wasted life. We have been given one life to make a difference for the Kingdom of God—to live full of freedom in Him and be joyfully filled with the fruit of right relationship with Him. These "enemies of the cross" have chosen waste over life. I understand Paul's heartbreak and weeping. We should all weep at the ultimate waste of what could and *should* have been. God has given us the freedom to choose Him or not—but ignoring the ultimate Gift ends in such tragedy.

To understand what leads to destruction, let's dig into the three aspects Paul outlines: "their god is their belly"; "they glory in their shame"; and their "minds [are] set on earthly things" (Philippians 3:19).

2. What do you think Paul means by "their god is their belly"? (Hint: Feel free to dig into the BLB with this one.)

We could go a few ways with this statement, really. Perhaps Paul is referring to clean versus unclean food, which—like circumcision—was a discussion as Jews and non-Jews became one in Christ (see Acts 15; Romans 14; 16:18; 1 Corinthians 8–10; Colossians 2:16). But as I look at the original Greek and the information in the *Interlinear* and *Lexicon* sections of the BLB, I wonder if Paul meant something more.

 ## *History Lesson*

As God was forming the Israelites into a nation, He provided laws that would set them apart from the cultures around them. That is where we first encounter this idea of clean versus unclean food. Though the lists in Leviticus 11 and Deuteronomy 14 don't mention every single creature on the earth, these passages provide guidelines for knowing which animals are fit and unfit (clean and unclean) for the Israelites to eat.

> 25 *You shall therefore separate the clean beast from the unclean, and the unclean bird from the clean. You shall not make yourselves detestable by beast or by bird or by anything with which the ground crawls, which I have set apart for you to hold unclean.* 26 *You shall be holy to me, for I the LORD am holy and have separated you from the peoples, that you should be mine.*
>
> LEVITICUS 20:25-26

Within this list are groupings of land animals, flying animals, water animals, insects, and crawling creatures. It's interesting to read, though part of me wonders, *Why, Lord? What's Your reasoning on allowing Your people to eat some creatures and not others?*

As I did some digging, I discovered that while yes, the clean/unclean guidelines were to set the Israelites apart as God's chosen people, God also provided these laws for their well-being (Deuteronomy 5:29). Every animal God deems

unclean tends to eat weak or diseased animals or consumes something that could sicken or kill us. For example,
shellfish—such as oysters, mussels, and clams—devour
decaying organic matter that sinks to the sea floor, including
sewage.[12]

But in Acts 10:9-16 God sets a new paradigm for His
people's relationship with food. In Acts 10:15, the Lord tells
Peter, "What God has made clean, do not call common." In
other words, the law that the Jewish people lived by in order to
be set apart as His chosen people no longer applied. The new
covenant wipes out this portion of the law. As Christians, we
can enjoy foods such as crab, shrimp, and pork (bacon!) that
our kosher friends do not.

This word for *belly* (in Philippians 3:19) is *koilia* (κοιλία, pronounced *koy-lee-ah*), which also means *appetite*. We often use that
word in a nonfood way, like when we say, "She has such an appetite
for life" to describe someone who embraces adventure and wonder,
right? But our appetites can also be negative, things that control us
and push us to unhealthy extremes—think gluttony and addiction,
for example. So perhaps that is what Paul is referring to—that these
enemies of the Cross are controlled by negative appetites.

But this *koilia* (κοιλία) word also refers to "the innermost part of
a [person], the soul, heart as the seat of thought, feeling, choice."[13]
We've been looking at the life that really matters, and here, as Paul
shows us the opposite of that kind of life, I wonder if he's also talking about the innermost thoughts and choices that drive the life of
rejecting God. What is the opposite of a life that emerges from the
goodness of Jesus? I immediately think of a term our pastor Nirup
Alphonse recently used as he preached on Galatians 6: *self-gospel*.

All throughout this letter to the Philippian church, we read
about *gospel* and *unity*. But what gospel are we living into? The
gospel of Jesus? Or a gospel focused on self?

3. What do you think is the difference between Jesus' gospel and the gospel of self?

Someone living a self-gospel thinks that the good news about life is the great things she's done. Sure, she says she's doing it all *for* Him, but in reality, it's about her image. Self-gospel relies heavily on list-making and an internal dialogue that says, *I'm doing so much for God. He's so lucky I'm on His team.* If we're not careful, our thoughts can start to sound like this:

Hey God, know what's awesome? The fact that I spent a whole forty-two minutes on this Bible study today.

Hey God, know who's selfless? I tithed 20 percent instead of 10 percent this week.

Hey God, know who's committed? I knew every single word of the worship songs at church on Sunday. I didn't even need to read a slide. And did you see my hands raised and my eyes closed? Longer than anybody else, Lord. I mean . . . not that I'd know . . . since my eyes were closed. I mean, mostly closed . . .

Self-gospel emerges from pride and a subconscious belief that somehow the things we do prove our worth and value to God and others. I do it. I suspect you do it too.

4. Where do you struggle with self-gospel—looking to yourself as the Good News? How would you fill out your internal dialogue?

Hey God,

Looking the part has everything to do with self-gospel. In fact, there are three aspects of *self* that fuse it all together:

a. self-performance;
b. self-promotion; and
c. self-preservation.

This third facet of self-preservation is a particularly dangerous one because it goes against everything Paul teaches on within the actual, *real* gospel of Jesus Christ. Self-preservation means we're always looking out for *numero uno*. But as Jesus followers, we're supposed to live counterculturally, embracing the Cross and the ultimate sacrifice of Jesus Himself—which means we'll face persecution and struggle just as He did.

5. How does self-preservation keep us from living out the true gospel?

In self-preservation, we may speak and even act in accordance with the way of Jesus . . . until it gets hard. This isn't just slipping up and making a poor decision. This is consistently choosing to act like everything depends on us and our ability to control our circumstances, living in sin and fear because we think we can't fully depend on God. When we live in self-preservation, we can even subconsciously decide that we'll come through "even if He doesn't."

Paul continues in Philippians 3:19, warning that these enemies "glory in their shame, with minds set on earthly things." This kind of enemy of God tosses aside morality, thinking that they have the right to do what they want, or that God will forgive them for whatever they do. One of my favorite commentaries on Philippians talks about this very thing:

> They had succumbed to a tendency known as antinomianism, i.e., a throwing off of the moral code and decent behaviour on the mistaken ground that the body was an irrelevance once the mind had been illumined and the soul redeemed. Hence moral restraints could be ignored, and no carnal sin could stain the pure soul.[14]

6. Have you ever felt tempted to continue in a sin because you know God's grace covers you? What are the dangers of that mindset?

As we talked about just a few days ago, God loves you just the way you are. And while this is true, it's not the whole story. When we limit God's love to a blanket covering over all of our behavior, we miss the depth and breadth of that love, His desire to craft us into people who are more like Him and live more authentic and restored lives.

We do not need to "clean ourselves up" before coming to God. But once we have laid all our dirt, grime, and baggage at His feet, we are to leave it with Him. We don't show God our junk and then pick it up again. That would be ridiculous. When we follow Him, He makes us a new creation. And new creations don't carry the junk and sin of their old selves.

As Paul reminds us in Philippians 3:20, our true inheritance is in heaven. Right now, we are resident aliens, exiles living for a time in a foreign place (Hebrews 11:13; James 1:1; 1 Peter 1:1; 2:11). We aren't enemies of the Cross. We are citizens of heaven. Let's stand firm in this reality (Philippians 4:1) and live in the longing for the full restoration of our Savior, Jesus Christ.

As you approach God today, humbly bring the parts of your life where you follow a self-gospel. Talk with the Lord about your struggle to fully give Him control. I have a feeling God has some loving words for you, so make sure you take time to listen to His response.

Amen.

WEEK 5 • *Notes*

Share your biggest takeaways from this week:

Live the Example

Philippians 4:2-9

WEEK 6 • *Day 1*

 READ PHILIPPIANS 4:2-3

I'm not a fan of drama. Reality TV stresses me out. When I pass the magazines in the grocery-store checkout, I feel old because I have no idea who most of the people on the covers are or why they're feuding. For me at least, life brings enough drama on its own, and the idea of taking on any more exhausts me. Today we see that Paul didn't love drama either—which is why he has some strong words for two women in the Philippian church who have definitely stirred some up.

After sharing expansive thoughts on unity, personal examples of Paul's friends who are living a life that really matters, and warnings against people who choose a different kind of life, Paul's about to get up-close-and-personal with the Philippian church. He knows these people well, after all. He now wants them to understand what all of this means for them, right where they are. And he starts by addressing these bickering women.

Maybe I'm nosy, but I want to know more about what's upsetting Euodia and Syntyche. Whatever it is, it's significant enough for Paul to call them out by name in a letter he knew would be read aloud to the entire congregation. I wonder what went through these women's minds as they heard their names paired with Paul's admonition to bury the hatchet and get back on the same page. Can you imagine every head turning to where the women stood during the reading, their faces flooding a bright pink?

1. Look back at Philippians 2:1-2. How do Paul's words there speak to Euodia and Syntyche here?

In Philippians 2:2, Paul spurs the church to complete his joy by "being of the same mind, having the same love, being in full accord and of one mind," and he uses a nearly identical Greek phrase in Philippians 4:2. The word he uses here translated as "to live in harmony" (*phroneō*; φρονέω, pronounced *fro-neh-oh*) is one of mutuality and equality. In other words, Paul doesn't take sides. He simply calls these two women to live in harmony.

This word *phroneō* (φρονέω) means "to have understanding, be wise," "to be of the same mind, i.e., agree together, cherish the same views, be harmonious."[1] Living in harmony doesn't just happen—it requires actions like pursuing wisdom and choosing to agree. Rather than allowing disunity to intensify, these women need to actively snuff out their conflict.

I love that Paul calls these women out but does not shame them. In fact, he specifically points out that these are women "who have labored side by side with me in the gospel . . . whose names are in the book of life" (Philippians 4:3). Euodia and Syntyche aren't charlatans or imposters aiming to corrupt the church but, as Paul points out, good and loving women who are simply in a season of conflict. For the health of the church and the continued work of the gospel, their behavior has to stop. Both good friends and good leaders recognize the importance of bringing bad decisions and poor behavior to light.

Paul may not have known specifically what was going on, but the Lord gave him the wisdom to know how to address it. Euodia and Syntyche likely knew they needed to heal their relationship but perhaps didn't know where to start or have the tools to do so. Paul was under no illusions that they would end their feud merely by deciding to do so. Rather than commanding them to "Get along!" and "Forgive!," he instead advocates on their behalf, enlisting the help of trusted friends.

Let's dig into the BLB here, because many translations don't do this passage justice. Unless you happen to be studying out of the King James or American Standard Version, your Bible likely won't use the word *yokefellow*, the person Paul is directly addressing in Philippians 3:3.

2. Please grab your phone, open the BLB app, and head to the *Interlinear* section of Philippians 4:3. What can you learn about the Greek origins of this word *yokefellow*?

 History Lesson

I don't know why, but the word *yokefellow* immediately makes me envision the man with the yellow hat from *Curious George*. Perhaps because it brings to mind the idea of patient friendship.

The origin of the word *yokefellow* helps us in understanding an intent that far surpasses our English words: friend, confidant, or companion. A yokefellow is literally two companions in a yoke together.[2] In 2 Corinthians 6:14, Paul uses this "yoke" metaphor while warning believers to not become "unequally yoked with unbelievers" through mismatched alliances.

A yoke is used in farming. In Paul's day, a heavy wooden frame would be fastened across the shoulders of oxen or horses, attaching them to a plow, cart, or wagon. Once the yoke was secured, the animals would push against it as they moved forward, creating leverage to pull the load. Two similarly sized animals were needed to pull evenly; mismatched yokefellows would result in too much work for the larger animal, while the smaller would take on very little of the load and responsibility. For success, each animal must work equally and in sync.

Paul uses this term in reference to the Philippian church to indicate living in unity and colaboring, taking on equal shares of the work. In other words, Paul and this yokefellow were fastened together in service to God. Whomever this yokefellow was, they were obviously a "true companion" (which is how many Bibles translate this term).

For me, though, it seems that *true friend* doesn't capture the breadth of *yokefellow*. Your yokefellow is your person, the one you can do life closely with. You lean on each other, sweating and toiling and helping one another as you work toward the same purpose: a harvest of faith. The shared goal of living out the gospel is why Paul warns us in 2 Corinthians 6:14 to not become yokefellows with those who don't believe in Jesus: We'd be moving out of sync, going in different directions with different intention and objectives.

Yes, *syzygos* (σύζυγος, pronounced *sood-zoo-gos*) is a Greek word that means "co-yoked," "comrade," and "partner,"[3] but because of the capitalization in some sources, it's possible *Syzygos* was an actual person.[4] Perhaps Paul used this person's name as a pun, as he does in Philemon 1:11. In this incredibly short letter (Philemon is only twenty-five verses!), Paul writes about a man named Onesimus, whose name means *profitable* or *useful*, and says, "Formerly he was useless to you, but now he is indeed useful to you and to me" (Philemon 1:11). We may be seeing a similar play on words here. If *Syzygos* was indeed a person, Paul may be playfully urging that person to live into his or her name as a yokefellow (alongside Clement and "the rest of [his] fellow workers") to help these women reconcile.

Disunity can be devastating anywhere, but among the people of God, so much more is at stake. As I read through commentaries on this passage, this sentence stuck out to me: "Where there is disunity inside there is bound to be defeat outside."[5]

3. Where do you see disunity in the church today? What defeats might we face as a result?

Unity between these two women was important because the church is the body of Christ, which is supposed to be a replica of the ideal—a heavenly body of believers. Division and disunity among believers are chinks in the chain of the church's armor against the world. Earlier in the letter to the Philippians, Paul petitioned the body (the church) to be "standing firm in one spirit, with one mind" (Philippians 1:27-28). Let's be on guard against unresolved conflict in our relationships with brothers and sisters in Christ, so we can stand together in the midst of a world that does not know Him.

Talk to the Lord about the yokefellows in your life. If you feel a sense of unity and common purpose with them, then thank the Lord for all they are and do. If you're out of sync, living with different intentions and objectives, thank the Lord for their friendship and continue to invest in them, but ask the Lord to also provide someone in your life who can help equally shoulder the yoke of the gospel.

Amen.

WEEK 6 • *Day 2*

 READ PHILIPPIANS 4:4-5

I was at the police station yesterday for five hours because a few months back, one of our kids did something they're massively regretting. Even amid the stress and pain, I'm sort of rejoicing. Not at the situation, but at the outcome. I've seen God's hand of kindness through the whole thing. It's given me a new way to show yet another child that my love is unwavering. And because of this junk we're surviving, we're truly closer than we've ever been.

Through the years of being a mom, and especially being a mom to kids with trauma, I've realized that sometimes life is hard and downright stinks. That doesn't mean we just wallow in the yuck of it all, though. No—we can learn to find joy in what we're facing . . . if we look at our hard situation as a way to draw us closer to one another and to Christ Himself. My family has been through a lot of difficult situations, and each of them has caused us to grow into a deeper, more significant love. Why? Because we kept rejoicing in the Lord through the hard.

Often, we think joy means manufacturing some sort of hollow cheeriness, making ourselves be happy. But that's not joy. Joy goes far deeper than our circumstances and our ability to force feelings. Joy emerges through the direction of our heart.

1. How would you explain the difference between joy and happiness?

An article I read on Compassion International's website provides a great distinction between joy and happiness:

> It's possible to feel joy in difficult times. Joy doesn't need a smile in order to exist, although it does feel better with one. Joy can share its space with other emotions—sadness, shame or anger. Happiness can't.
>
> Happiness is not present in darkness and difficulty. Joy never leaves it. Joy undergirds our spirits; it brings to life peace and contentment.
>
> Joy requires a connection. . . . Joy is present. In the moment. Happiness mostly just passes through.[6]

Paul says to "rejoice in the Lord always"—*always* means during all seasons, no matter the situation. And while this word *rejoice* (*chairō*; χαίρω, pronounced *kai-roh*) does obviously mean "to . . . be glad," "to be 'cheer'ful," and to "joyfully" rejoice, it also goes so much deeper: "to . . . thrive."[7]

As soon as I read this in the BLB, I thought immediately about the Israelites in Jeremiah 29. At this point in history, God's people were suffering in captivity in Babylon and were falling into deep despair. Yet, through the prophet Jeremiah, God told them to do something that seemed crazy: thrive right where they were. *Yes,* life was hard. *Yes,* they had lost so much. *Yes,* they wanted peace and restoration. But despite all this, God wanted them to grow deep roots in the difficult season they were in:

⁵ Build houses and make yourselves at home.

Put in gardens and eat what grows in that country.

⁶ Marry and have children. Encourage your children to marry and have children so that you'll thrive in that country and not waste away.

⁷ Make yourselves at home there and work for the country's welfare.

Pray for Babylon's well-being. If things go well for Babylon, things will go well for you.

JEREMIAH 29:5-7, MSG

Usually when we recite Jeremiah 29:11—"'For I know the plans I have for you,' declares the LORD, 'plans to prosper you and not to harm you, plans to give you hope and a future'" (NIV)—we forget (or don't know) the bigger context. We desire joy, but don't want to have to go into exile to receive it. We want a relationship with Christ, but we aren't willing to take the time out of our busy schedules to be with Him. We choose things over God, just as the Israelites did all those years ago. What we must remember is that how we handle hardship and interruptions will affect our future. We need to recognize what determines our joy.

God allows things to happen so we can draw close to Him in them, and even in those hard seasons, He wants us to thrive. Free-falling may feel like death, but He patiently and calmly waits to catch us. For the Israelites, their pain meant something. As they learned to thrive, God would fully restore and reestablish them.

2. How does God's instruction to a captive Israel in Jeremiah 29 connect with Paul's command in Philippians 4 to rejoice in all things?

If we want to live with joy, we can't let our difficult situation or season absorb and overwhelm us. We need to step out and continue living.

How do we do that? Here's a little secret I've figured out over many years of hard: *How you think about God ultimately directs the stability and consistency of your joy.*

3. After telling us to rejoice in the Lord, what does Paul tell us to do? (Hint: See Philippians 4:5.)

"Let your reasonableness [or gentle spirit] be known." The word used here is *epieikēs* (ἐπιεικής, pronounced *eh-pee-ay-kays*), which is translated as "gentle," "patient," "equitable," and "fair."[8] In ancient Greek, this word often referred to responding with kindness when the normal or expected reaction was retaliation. Choosing to respond with gentleness when people might expect us to fight back seems upside down. Paul is talking about a kind of joy and a kind of living that upends all the normal ways of doing things. This way of life seems impossible—which is why the *focus* of our rejoicing matters.

4. When Paul reminds us to rejoice, he's not talking about rejoicing in a double scoop of ice cream or a pay raise. What are we to rejoice in?

Rejoice in the Lord. Paul even says it twice because he wants us to get this! Rejoicing in the Lord means having joy in Someone who is constant and never-changing. God is always loving, always present, always good, and always understanding. He's trustworthy enough to rejoice in *always.*

Hardships often prepare ordinary
people for extraordinary destiny.

C. S. LEWIS

When we know our heavenly Father deeply—when our knowledge of Him and relationship with Him grow and become richer through every circumstance—we can rejoice in Him through dark times and through light. God is in control. He can make beauty out of ashes (Isaiah 61:3). And because of that, we can rejoice in Him despite everything else.

Paul's not asking you to rejoice in the affair that's tearing your family apart. Or in the cancer that's ripping through your body or a loved one's. And I don't have to rejoice at my child's horrible decision-making. But you and I *can* rejoice in the Lord. In all things. No matter what. And if we can do that, we can't help but thrive.

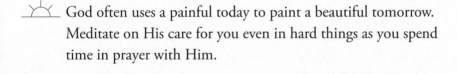 God often uses a painful today to paint a beautiful tomorrow. Meditate on His care for you even in hard things as you spend time in prayer with Him.

Amen.

WEEK 6 • *Day 3*

 READ PHILIPPIANS 4:6-7

I love storms. Like looove them. Not storms that are destructive, of course, like tsunamis, hurricanes, or tornadoes. But a good snow-storm or thunderstorm? I'm a happy girl. Whenever the rain pours down and the thunder and lightning party together in the sky, I open up our doors and windows so I can marvel at the sights and sounds.

When our two oldest boys were younger, they loved these down-pours too. Stripping off their clothes (I'd have to remind them that underwear was not optional), they'd run out onto the street in front of our home and dance, stomping their feet, splashing, and wav-ing their arms. These two sons are from very different regions of Ethiopia, but this dance of thankfulness for the rain was a tradition in both of their villages. Once their English language skills developed enough, they'd both tell us how much their communities prayed for rain. Droughts meant death, but rain meant life . . . and celebration. Prayer was a longing for life.

Why do we pray? Do we go before God only when we're desper-ate or need something? Do we pray sporadically, or does our prayer life feel dry and rote? Even harder, do we honestly and truly want to meet God in prayer . . . but right now it feels like we're talking to a blank wall?

Prayer seems like it should be so simple, and yet so many of us struggle with it. Paul's words in Philippians today get straight to the heart of prayer—but if we're honest, what he says about prayer can seem a bit daunting.

Here is the reality of prayer, though: God wants us to meet Him with everything we're going through because we can't live life based on our own doings. He is not out of reach or inaccessible. Prayer stimulates conversation between us and the Creator of the universe, closing the gap created by sin and propelling us into transformation. The life of prayer Paul describes is one of walking with God, hand in hand—and that life is one each of us can have.

Here in Philippians 4:6, Paul tells us to do several things:

- Do not be anxious
- Let your requests be made known
- Come before the throne with thanksgiving

1. What happens if we do this? (Hint: Philippians 4:7 tells us.)

When we come to God with expectant hearts of faith, thanking Him for what He has done and what He *will* do, we can lay down the anxiety that tries to overwhelm us with all the what-ifs. Thanksgiving before action shows faith that God will move.

Thanking Him for doing something you're not sure if He will actually do feels scary sometimes. After all, just because we're praying for a specific outcome doesn't mean it's the outcome God has in mind.

2. When was the last time you prayed something big and important, full of expectation and thankfulness?

We often say that the Lord gives us one of three answers when we pray: *yes, no,* or *wait.* Sometimes He speaks with more detail and depth, but often, the responses are just that simple. More than that, there are four ways that God speaks when He does answer:

- **Hear:** The Holy Spirit will whisper something to your heart, almost audibly.
- **Feel:** The Lord will speak to you with powerful emotion.
- **See:** The Lord will speak to you through visions or dreams.
- **Know:** The Lord will speak to you through strong thoughts, giving you no doubt that it's from Him.

3. Share a time when God spoke to you in one of these four ways. Did He give you a yes, no, or wait?

_____

_____

_____

_____

_____

A dear friend of mine recently found out she and her husband are unable to conceive. In vitro isn't even a viable option. She's devastated. He's crushed. God gave them a no that they weren't expecting. When things like this occur, it's okay to grieve. It's okay to have a time to lament, to mourn. Maybe God has said no to your loved one's healing. Maybe He's said no to the restoration of your marriage. Maybe He's closed the door on a dream you've held on to for as long as you can remember. Whatever this *thing* is, it's important to you. Having a time to weep and mourn the loss is okay. But even through that no, even through the grief, you can hold tight to this truth: The Lord has a purpose for His answer. He has a good and perfect plan (Jeremiah 29:11), even if it doesn't unfold in the time and the way you wish it would.

> As for God, his way is perfect:
>   The LORD's word is flawless;
>   he shields all who take refuge in him.
> PSALM 18:30, NIV

No matter the answer, we need to remember that as we pray with a heart full of expectation and thankfulness, meeting God in trust and prayer will give us an inexplainable peace. Peace isn't just the inverse of not being anxious; it's the guard *against* anxiety.

4. How do you think peace guards against anxiety? What might that look like in your life?

_____

_____

_____

_____

_____

_____

It is absolutely imperative at the outset that you come to terms with this simple yet life-changing truth: *God is for you.* If you don't believe that, then you'll pray small timid prayers. If you do believe it, then you'll pray big audacious prayers. And one way or another, your small timid prayers or big audacious prayers will change the trajectory of your life and turn you into two totally different people. Prayers are prophecies. They are the best predictors of your spiritual future. *Who you become* is determined by *how you pray.* Ultimately, the transcript of your prayers becomes the script of your life.[9]

MARK BATTERSON

Sometimes we are so devastated by our painful circumstances that we have very little faith left. We feel like we're running on fumes. In these times, prayer can be profoundly difficult. *Is God listening? Will He act?*

5. Head to Mark 9:14-29 and read the story of the father of the demon-possessed son. What do we see here about meeting Jesus in prayer when trusting Him is hard?

"I believe; help my unbelief!" Sometimes I've felt such immense despair that praying these words were all my heart could utter. Coming to God in thankful expectation doesn't mean we're whistling and clicking our heels in bliss. We may be flat on the floor, face in the carpet as we ugly cry. But every time I've genuinely handed my request over to Him, every time I've chosen to believe that He will work, even if it's in a way I may not want . . . He has met me with peace. The crisis hasn't physically shifted, but now I'm looking toward the light of God rather than the darkness of the situation. The peace of God that surpasses all understanding is the fruit that grows out of prayer.

If you struggle with prayer, or if you have been hurt by any of God's answers, talk to Him about that. Tell Him if you're unsure what to say half the time or if you feel like your words hit the ceiling and fall back down to earth. The Lord wants conversation just as much as we crave it. Lay it all out there. You want to have the desire to pray more? Talk with Him about it. Want to become a prayer warrior? Tell Him that, too. When your heart and His are in perfect alignment, He will absolutely give you anything you ask (Psalm 37:4).

Amen.

WEEK 6 • *Day 4*

 READ PHILIPPIANS 4:8-9

In most parts of life, I've wanted a manual for success. You know, like $A + B = C$. When I was pregnant, I read all the parenting books: how to get your baby onto a great sleep schedule right away, how to get your child to eat healthy, how to get them to obey when asked the first time. Strangely, I wasn't as successful and perfect as I expected once I was in the throes of real life.

Although parenting, marriage, and business-related advice can be helpful, sadly, $A + B$ just doesn't equal C every single time. Life is unpredictable, and human wisdom is unreliable. But you know what we can rely on? Biblical promises.

In today's passage, Paul gives us an *if this, then that* recommendation for life. With this, he's saying $A + B = C$ . . . Every. Single. Time!

1. I'm the absolute *worst* at math, but let's pretend I'm the math nerd I've always wanted to be! Ready for a little equation? We're going to start backwards, with Paul's C (the conclusion or outcome). If we add his $A + B$, what do we receive? (Hint: C is found at the very end of verse 9.)

The outcome Paul is talking about is the peace of God. (Tomorrow we're going to spend all our time on the concept of peace, so we're just going to lightly touch on it now.) Now that we know the solution (*C*) is peace, let's figure out the rest.

Let's start with *A*.

2. What are the eight things that Paul shares with us in Philippians 4:8?

a. _____

b. _____

c. _____

d. _____

e. _____

f. _____

g. _____

h. _____

Now we're at: *whatever is . . . true, honorable, just, pure, lovely, commendable, excellent, worthy of praise* + *B* = *God's peace.*

3. So, what is *B*?

_____

_____

_____

The answer to what *B* is emerges from both verses. In Philippians 4:8, Paul says to think about these eight things, and in Philippians 4:9, Paul instructs us to practice these things. When we set our minds on these things *and* put them into practice, God's peace will be with us.

4. Turn in your Bibles to James 1:22-25 and Matthew 7:24-27. How do these two passages connect with Paul's command to not only set our minds on whatever is true, honorable, just, pure, and the like, but to live into those things?

The verb used for *think* in Philippians 4:8—*logizomai* (λογίζομαι, pronounced *lo-gid-zo-mai*)—means "to deliberate," "weigh, meditate on."[10] In other words, *we need to think rightly because the harvest of our thoughts influences the way life will be lived.*

5. Where might God be calling you to change your thinking? How could that influence your actions?

J. Alec Motyer says in his commentary on Philippians,

We are to meditate on, to prize as valuable, and to be influenced by all that is *true*, all that merits serious thought and encourages serious-mindedness, all that accords with justice and moral purity, all that is fragrant and *lovely*, all that brings with it a good word, that speaks well, whatever has genuine worth of any sort and merits *praise*.[11]

Following Jesus isn't just about thinking the right things. Who He is and what He has done should change us in thought *and* in action. And as we put into practice the life He calls us to, we will find ourselves surrounded by His peace, no matter what we're facing. How beautiful is that?

 Spend some time talking with the Lord about your desire to be a woman whose eyes are set on *whatever is true, honorable, just, pure, lovely, commendable, excellent, and worthy of praise*. This is the sort of reputation I want to have and the kind of legacy I want to leave . . . and I have a feeling you do too!

_____
_____
_____
_____
_____
_____
_____
_____
_____

Amen.

WEEK 6 • *Day 5*

READ PHILIPPIANS 4:7-9

One thing I love about Ethiopian culture is their greetings. In Europe, you'll get a singular kiss—or perhaps two—on the cheek. In the country several of my children were born in, the country we have fallen head-over-heels for, you receive three. In fact, if you haven't seen someone in a while, sometimes you'll get four or five or more!

Along with offering this sweet kiss greeting (which our girls especially love), I've learned to say, "Selam tena yistilign," which essentially means, *May God give you peace and health*. But because my accent is wildly horrible (or maybe I'm just *fearful* that it is), I mostly greet my Ethiopian friends with a smile and a simple *selam—peace*.

If you have any Jewish friends, you'll likely hear the word *shalom* frequently in greetings and blessings. Though this Hebrew word is translated as "peace be with you," there's more to it than that. Holistically, *shalom* encompasses physical, spiritual, social, and psychological well-being: right with God, right with(in) oneself, and right with others.[12]

Shalom is the word typically used for peace in the Old Testament. For example, check out Psalm 85:8:

> Let me hear what God the LORD will speak,
>> for he will speak peace to his people, to his saints;
>> but let them not turn back to folly.

1. Look up this verse in the BLB and open the *Interlinear*. What does *shalowm* (שָׁלוֹם, pronounced *sha-lom*) mean?

How does this help us as we read Paul's words about peace in Philippians 4? Because while we find completeness, health, prosperity, safety, and peace with God all over the Bible, this isn't the same peace we're talking about in Paul's letter.[13]

Or is it?

The Old Testament is largely written in Hebrew, the language spoken in ancient Palestine. (In the nineteenth and twentieth centuries, "it was revived as a spoken language" and is currently Israel's official language.[14]) As you know, though, Philippians was written entirely in ancient Greek, as was the whole New Testament. The difference in language obviously means different characters, words, and meanings.

And as we look again at Philippians 4, verses 7 and 9, in the BLB, we see that the New Testament Greek uses the word *eirēnē*.

2. What does *eirēnē* (εἰρήνη, pronounced *ay-ray-nay*) mean?

As you've likely noticed, these two words mean largely the same thing. And in both cases, the English word *peace* really doesn't capture what's going on. The peace of *eirēnē* takes on much of what is included in *shalom*, such as restoration and wholeness. *Eirēnē* doesn't just take that which is broken and fix it; instead, this peace makes the broken whole and new. That's what the gospel is all about!

> Peace I leave with you; my peace I give to you. Not as the world gives do I give to you. Let not your hearts be troubled, neither let them be afraid.
> JOHN 14:27

We can go to counseling and read self-help books. We can read every beautiful faith-based book on the shelf. We can even read the Bible itself cover to cover, over and over. But unless we have given our hearts over to Christ, we will only be making ourselves better. Only He can make us new. This peace, this *eirēnē*, is every believer being made new. Not because we deserve it, but because God really is in the restoration business.

I just received a text from our adult son and my heart broke as he shared some hard things he's experiencing right now, especially concerning a close friend who was in a tragic car accident this week.

Peace is something my sweet son needs right now, so I took a break from digging into this verse as he and I voice texted while he's at work, unable to focus. But because God's timing is impeccable, this verse was at the forefront of my mind as we talked. I created a quick graphic of Philippians 4:6-7 and texted it to him so he could put it on the lock screen of his phone for a visual reminder of the encouragement Paul shares with us. As we continue into this passage, we find how to have this peace we all so desperately yearn for. And exactly how *is* that? Well . . . we need to fill our minds with certain things.

This promise of peace surrounds a verse you may find familiar: Philippians 4:8. The call of where to rest our thoughts is the path to peace.

3. Look up Philippians 4:8 in several translations and pen it down in your favorite. In my opinion, the word *adelphos* (ἀδελφός, pronounced *ah-del-fos*) in Philippians 4:8 is better translated as *brethren*, not *brother*. According to my thesaurus, brethren includes all kin and relatives, beyond simply a male sibling. So add the word *sisters* to the beginning if your translation hasn't already—these words are for us, too!

Over a decade ago, I found an oval-shaped, hand-lettered sign with these words and hung it on the wall at the base of our staircase at our home in San Antonio. I read Philippians 4:8-9 every single time I hustled down the stairs while running late (per usual). I read them as I bounced a screaming infant on my hip, about to cry myself from my own exhaustion. I read them while Ben and I carried arms full of dirty clothes down the stairs, dropping stray socks like petals behind us. I never got tired of that sign. I'd notice it and read it each time I came eye to eye with it on that staircase.

I think Paul's words here stick with us—we're all in need of peace. And when we concentrate on living a life exhibiting these characteristics, how could we *not* have more peace in our lives?

Think about these things:

- whatever is true (authentic and genuine)
- whatever is honorable (reputable and virtuous in character)
- whatever is just (honest and upright)
- whatever is pure (clean and uncontaminated)
- whatever is lovely (pleasing and beautifully captivating)
- whatever is commendable (gracious and of good repute)
- anything excellent (admirable and exemplary)
- anything worthy of praise (worthy of celebration and appreciation)

Of course, when we get to Paul's words in Philippians 4:9, we might think he's being cocky, bragging that he's attained a level of holiness and righteousness we can only dream about. After all, if I told you to practice what you have learned, received, heard, and seen in me, I'd sound incredibly arrogant, right? But somehow, it's different here.

4. Turn in your Bibles to 1 Corinthians 11:1. How does this verse help us understand that Paul isn't being egocentric here in Philippians 4?

Paul is saying that this peace is not out of reach. We all follow the example of Christ. He equips us to live in this place of right thinking,

LIVE THE EXAMPLE   •   203

of anything that is excellent and praiseworthy, through the way we live and breathe and move. And as we do that, the God of peace is with us. God's peace is for us. God's peace was for Paul, a man who once persecuted God's people. God's peace was for the Philippians. And God's peace is for each of us.

As you spend time talking to the Lord, work up a plan together on how you can make Philippians 4:8 part of your real life. How can you face the direction of peace and loveliness, rather than compromise and selfishness? Where do you struggle to think about anything honorable and worthy of praise, and how can you distance yourself from those situations? Ask God to design your life to pursue peace.

Amen.

WEEK 6 • *Notes*

Share your biggest takeaways from this week:

The Lord's Provision

Philippians 4:10-23

WEEK 7 • *Day 1*

 READ PHILIPPIANS 4:10-12

The past few years, my friends have teased me that my life is intentionally contained to a five-mile radius. Kids' schools, church, gym, after-school and weekend activities—everything in a nice, neat little bubble where I didn't commute much and hardly ever dealt with traffic. That was then. This year, because our kids are older and things are now spread out, my sweet little bubble has been ripped to shreds. I spend at least three hours in the car each day and have told our kids I'm saving up for a helicopter.

Now, not all of this being-stuck-in-the-car stuff is bad. I get to have great conversations with my sweet kids because they have no one to talk to but me (thanks to our great rule of *no phones out in the car*). I also get to listen to Audible and many (*many!*) podcasts.

Each of these seasons—the life-in-a-radius and life-in-the-car—have their great parts and their hard parts. And I've had to learn what it is to rest in God in the midst of the ups and downs of both. Paul talks about this kind of thing (times a thousand, if you think about his ups and downs) in today's verses:

> ¹¹ Not that I am speaking of being in need, for I have learned in whatever situation I am to be content. ¹² I know how to be brought low, and I know how to abound.
>
> PHILIPPIANS 4:11-12

The word *content* (*autarkēs*; αὐτάρκης, pronounced *aw-tar-kays*) means self-sufficient. Wait, what? *Self*-sufficient? I thought we're supposed to be *God*-sufficient. Are you confused here too? This is the only time in the entire Bible this word is used. Go ahead and jump to the BLB so we can dig into this one together.

1. Go to the *Interlinear* for Philippians 4:11 and pen down what you learn about the word *content*:

_____

_____

_____

If we scroll through the definitions and the lexicons, we'll see stuff like "contented with one's lot, with one's means" . . . but how does that tie into the idea of being "sufficient for one's self, strong enough or possessing enough to need no aid or support"?[1]

2. What do you think Paul means by using this word here?

_____

_____

_____

Honestly, I've spent a couple of hours researching this. You should see all the books I have open on my desk and the Google tabs open on my laptop! I'm just not receiving a clear answer. But as I've been praying and talking to the Lord about what He wants me to take away from this word, this is what He's pointing me toward:

Paul's contentment and self-sufficiency aren't focused on *self* but rather on not needing anything he doesn't already have. He is "strong enough or possessing enough to need no aid or support" because he already has all he needs in Christ!

When we have all we need in Christ, we aren't looking for more. I'm reminded by something John Piper wrote in his book *Future Grace*:

> It's obvious then that covetousness is exactly the opposite of faith. It's the loss of contentment in Christ so that we start to crave other things to satisfy the longings of our hearts. And

there's no mistaking that the battle against covetousness is a battle against unbelief.[2]

Contentment is void of covetousness because covetousness leads us to look for more outside of Jesus.

Covetousness sounds like such a greedy word, but so often there's real pain and longing behind it. Many times, we find ourselves struggling in a season we don't want to be in. Maybe our friends, family members, coworkers, or even people we follow online are receiving what we've been praying for and are living the life *we* want (marriage, babies, beautiful homes, successful businesses). During these seasons, contentment is hard and covetousness creeps in. How can we cling to Christ when our ache feels overwhelming?

3. Where do you ache? Where does Jesus not feel like enough?

On my dear friend Mary Marantz's podcast, her friend Natalie shared about her way through this.[3] Natalie is a solopreneur and has coined a beautiful concept called #communityovercompetition. But as she struggled with a brain tumor, infertility, and her life looking different from how she expected it to, she realized that if she genuinely believed in that concept, she needed to believe it in *all* aspects of her life, not just in her career. God has created us so that serotonin and dopamine are released into our brains as we concentrate on what we're thankful for, causing joy and hope and growth—and in her seasons of pain, Natalie wanted to overflow with gratefulness.

With incredible intentionality, every time Natalie received a baby-shower invitation in the mail or heard of yet another friend entering a season she longed for, she allowed herself to feel the pain. But instead of falling to the ground weeping or becoming bitter, she would praise the Lord for her friend and her friend's child, allowing a heart of thankfulness to grow. On a daily basis, Natalie shifted her mind away from her pain, away from what she didn't have, and instead turned toward the many blessings she had already received. She realized that contentment meant trusting God with her life because there is no such thing as scarcity in the Kingdom of God.

> *Scarcity says, I must be better than her.*
> *Abundance says, there is enough room*
> *for both of us to shine.*[4]
> NATALIE FRANKE

When someone else gets that *thing* we've been praying for, it feels like we can't breathe. Not because we don't want what's best for them—we truly do. But sometimes we forget that in God's economy, we both can win. He is going to use us in different but redemptive and life-giving ways.

4. Do you think contentment and abundance go hand in hand? Why or why not?

Contentment means seeing abundance when our eyes are turned upward. Paul wasn't in a place of earthly abundance while chained to a guard. And yet we see incredible abundance of joy and gratitude through his entire letter to the Philippians. In Philippians 4:11, we are reminded that circumstances didn't affect Paul's love of God or gratitude for life. He lived from a place of thankfulness no matter the season or circumstance.

5. How does what we learned about Philippians 4:7-9 last week tie into this contentment we're learning about today?

_____

_____

_____

To genuinely achieve what Paul is asking of us here in verses 10-12, we must allow God to shift our perspective to His bigger plan that will bring glory to His Kingdom and to His story through us. There is purpose behind every one of God's *no* or *wait* answers. If we dwell on and practice all the things we read about in Philippians 4:8 and come to Him with prayers full of thanksgiving (Philippians 4:6), then His beautiful, unexplainable peace will be with us—and we will be content.

Talk with the Lord about where you have been living with a mentality of scarcity. Ask Him to help you rest in what He has given you so you can cheer on others in what He has given them.

_____

_____

_____

_____

_____

_____

_____

_____

_____

_____

Amen.

WEEK 7 • *Day 2*

 READ PHILIPPIANS 4:12-13

When our kids were really little, my husband, Ben, went to a class about keeping children safe from sexual assault. The incredible angel of a woman who taught the class is named Feather, and she has dedicated her life to helping people parent safe children. One of our big takeaways from Feather's class and book is that our children should understand we don't keep secrets—we keep surprises.

> **Surprise:** *Meant to be kept quiet about temporarily, then share the surprise and people are happy.*

> **Secret:** *Meant to be kept quiet forever, often to protect something that would make people unhappy.*

> FEATHER BERKOWER

Paul's secret, though, isn't like that. The word *secret* in verse 12 is often not translated well because our English language doesn't have a perfect word to interpret it. Paul isn't trying to keep something a secret. He's not saying that he's found the answer but needs to keep it quiet. That would certainly hinder the very thing he's trying to do in sharing the gospel, right?

1. Let's head to Philippians 4:12 in the *Interlinear* of the BLB and tap on the phrase *I have learned the secret*. How else is *myeō* (μυέω, pronounced *moo-eh-oh*) translated?

What Paul had discovered was the answer to a puzzle, a mystery he hadn't perceived before. This phrase has nothing to do with secrecy and everything to do with teaching—and as we know, Paul was a fantastic teacher.

2. So, what is this mystery (or surprise!) that he has learned from facing plenty and hunger, abundance and need?

I'm just as happy with little as with much, with much as with little. I've found the recipe for being happy whether full or hungry, hands full or hands empty.

PHILIPPIANS 4:12, MSG

I love how this is worded in *The Message*. The word *recipe* is a perfect word illustration, because Paul is explaining to his Philippian friends (and us) the right technique and ingredients that will bring forth contentedness and strength.

3. What does Paul say in Philippians 4:13?

This is going to sound rather elementary, but I think you need to hear it as much as I've needed the reminder: *all things*. Not just easy things! Not just things that are familiar or comfortable or simple. We can do *anything* in the strength of Jesus.

Scared about something? God gives you strength.

Don't feel up to the task? God gives you strength.

Don't know how to do it? God gives you strength.

Hurting and breaking in two? God gives you strength.

4. What would you say are the two key words within the phrase *I can do all things in Him who strengthens me*?

If you said the words *in Him*, then you're spot on! Think back on Israel and the first Passover. When God's chosen people painted lamb's blood over their doorposts, they were *in* the blood of the lamb as they resided within their house that night. In other words, they were sheltered because they were *in Him*. Likewise, now that Jesus has come as the Lamb and ultimate sacrifice, we also find shelter in Him. As J. A. Motyer comments,

> This relationship of being "in Christ" . . . is something we enjoy by consciously attending to it. . . . Just as a chick runs to the mother hen for protection, so he runs to God. In the same way Paul, and we ourselves, are "in Christ" by fleeing to him, and pressing close to him, covering ourselves in him, hiding in him, by seeing the danger and taking shelter in him.[5]

As we are in Christ, not only will He be our strength, as we read in Psalm 46:1—"God is our refuge and strength"—but as Paul tells us, He strengthens us. So what does it look like to be women of strength?

My friend Ashley is a woman of strength. Five days a week, she wakes up when it's still dark and drives the twenty-or-so minutes to her CrossFit gym. She's trained her body to do some incredible things. I mean, she does headstand push-ups, which are literally push-ups . . . while you're doing a headstand! But here's the thing: She didn't just decide to show up one day and crank ten of those babies out. She also doesn't just show up (or not) whenever she feels like it. She is committed and works daily toward this goal of strength.

God offers strength—we've seen it through Paul and throughout Scripture. But living into that strength doesn't mean just passively receiving it. It means commitment to living in Him. Intentionality. Consistency.

According to my ESV translation, the Bible contains 228 references to the word *strength* or some variation of it. An in-depth study of this powerful word could fill an entire book. But as I opened my Bible to the concordance at the back, and my finger ran down verse after verse containing *strength*, I found myself struck by one passage in particular: Proverbs 31:25.

5. Flip over to Proverbs 31:25 and write it below. And if it's been a while since you've read all of Proverbs 31 (or if you never have), then I encourage you to go through the whole thing before continuing.

This passage was written not as a description of a specific woman, but as a list of qualities for a man to look for in a future wife. In fact, the mother of a king named Lemuel spoke this wisdom over him.

In these verses, we read that the woman's strength and dignity are so thick, she can wrap it around herself as clothing that will keep her warm. She is savvy, hardworking, unafraid of the future. But this passage isn't meant to make us women feel shame or less than or not enough—remember, the woman didn't actually exist. We simply see a broad and beautiful list of the different ways we women can live out goodness and wisdom—different pictures of what it looks like to be a woman of "noble character" (Proverbs 31:10, NIV).

6. Type Proverbs 31:25 in the BLB, head to the *Interlinear* section, and tap on the word *strength*. What does 'oz (עֹז, pronounced *oze*) mean? (Check out the lexicons, too!)

I absolutely love the descriptions of "boldness," "loud," and "mighty." This woman sounds like a warrior, doesn't she? And if we read all the way down into *Gesenius' Hebrew-Chaldee Lexicon*, we get even more of that picture with phrases like "strength, might, power used of God." And "vehemence of anger," "heroes," "defense, refuge, protection" as well as "a firm, secure, fortified tower."[6] I mean, all of this in one simple word that the English language deems merely *strength*? This woman lives a life of intention and is certainly not to be trifled with.

7. If you were using these words and characteristics above, how would you describe a woman of strength?

_____

_____

_____

_____

_____

Read through what you just wrote and draw a little star above each description that you feel does *not* portray you. Remember, this is not a sign of less than! We are all growing, all works in progress, and knowing the kind of woman we want to be helps each of us aim in the right direction.

Now, circle anything that *does* portray you. It's okay—this isn't bragging. No one but you and God are looking at what you're doing right now. He does not want us to downplay our strengths but rather to feel confident in how He's created us.

True strength is not about doing—it's about trusting. Only through trusting the Lord can we be truly strong. As we trust Him, listen to Him, and strive to be like Him, we'll grow stronger. Our spiritual, emotional, and mental muscles will begin to grow.

Talk with the Lord about how you can be more intentional in building your strength, whether physically, mentally, emotionally, or spiritually. Our heavenly Father created you with all of these facets and cares about each and every one.

_____

_____

_____

_____

_____

_____

_____

_____

_____

_____

Amen.

WEEK 7 • *Day 3*

READ PHILIPPIANS 4:14-18

The members of the church in Philippi, as we well know at this point, are dear friends of the apostle Paul. And though they're unable to carry his physical burdens, they are able to share his trouble in a relational and spiritual way. Think of the bond that forms when you can support someone you love through a hard time. Maybe you sat with a friend during their cancer treatments. Maybe they sat with you after the death of your spouse or parent. Ben and I are fused together even closer every time our children's pain and trauma rears its ugly head, when they're in an accident, or when they're hurt by a racist attack at school.

THE LORD'S PROVISION • 217

Your experiences are likely different, but pain is pain and struggle is struggle—and coming alongside one another in love, taking on a bit of the pain, only brings us closer in relationship. If we choose not to let solitude step in, not to try to bear the weight alone, others can step into the pain with us, just as the Philippians did for Paul.

This coming alongside is just what Paul is talking about when he says the Philippians shared in his trouble (Philippians 4:14). The Greek word for *share* (*sygkoinōneō*; συγκοινωνέω, pronounced *soon-koi-noh-neh-oh*) is translated basically how you'd expect: "to become a partaker together with others, or to have fellowship with a thing."[7]

1. But let's look closer at the two root words that make up *sygkoinōneō* (συγκοινωνέω). Opening the *Interlinear* in the BLB for Philippians 4:14, look at the Root Word (Etymology) entry. What are these two words, and what do they mean?

Syn (σύν, pronounced *soon*) denotes "union" or "companionship," right?[8] And what about *koinōneō* (κοινωνέω, pronounced *koi-noh-neh-oh*)? Does this one sound familiar? If you've done much digging in the Bible before, you may recognize how similar this word is to *koinonia*, which is used all over the New Testament in noun and verb forms (twenty times, in fact!). *Koinonia* is significant for many reasons, but largely because the first use of it was in Acts 2, shortly after the coming of the Holy Spirit.[9] *Koinonia* was a togetherness, a commonality in devotion to Christ and living on life-or-death mission together.

*[The koinonia] is an all-in, life-or-death
collective venture in the face of great evil and
overwhelming opposition. True fellowship is
less like friends gathered to watch the Super
Bowl and more like players on the field in
blood, sweat, and tears, huddled in the
backfield only in preparation for the next
down. True fellowship . . . is more the invading
troops side by side on the beach at Normandy
than it is the gleeful revelers
in the street on V-E Day.*[10]

DAVID MATHIS

This blood-sweat-and-tears kind of togetherness and unity is what Paul recognizes in his relationship with the Philippian church. It's what happens when we move beyond the meet-and-greet at church and allow vulnerability and action to infuse our relationships.

How did the Philippian church do this for Paul, even though they were far from where he was imprisoned in Rome? Well, remember Epaphroditus? The reason he was sent to see Paul in the first place was to give him a gift. We learned earlier in our study that during Paul's in-between time in Rome, while he was charged but not yet convicted, he lived in a rented house in Rome under house arrest. He may have had an open door so all could come to see him, but he needed things in order to live—things that were only supplied by outside assistance, not the Roman prison system. We don't know exactly what Epaphroditus brought from the Philippian church, other than offering himself as a helper (although it is widely assumed the gift was at least in part financial), but we do know the church's assistance was imperative to Paul's health and survival.

2. The Philippian church was close to Paul's heart for many reasons, but what is one specific cause for his love and admiration of this body of believers? (Hint: See Philippians 4:15.)

No church other than the Philippian body entered into partnership with Paul in receiving and giving! This is crazy to me. Paul had poured out to churches all over Asia and Europe, but only this church gave back. And we see in Philippians 4:16 that this isn't the only time they had done so (it even says *once and again*, meaning they gave multiple times).

3. Why do you think no one else supported Paul?

Back in Philippians 1:17, we read that other churches and believers were benefiting from Paul's imprisonment, muddling things up and instigating *thlipsis* (θλῖψις, pronounced *thlip-sis*), which means "anguish," "affliction," "trouble," "burdened," and "pressure (literally or figuratively)."[11] Sadly, the church as a whole had yet to comprehend the concept of openhearted, sacrificial, generous, altruistic giving. Something I read in Ian Cron and Suzanne Stabile's *The Road Back to You* captures this dynamic perfectly:

Self-interested giving expects payback, whereas altruistic giving comes without any strings attached. As the saying goes,

"When you give and expect a return, that's an investment. When you give and don't expect anything back, that's love."[12]

In Mark 12:41-44 and Luke 21:1-4, we read about the poor widow who gave all she had. It's a significant story that teaches us the importance of faith-filled, sacrificial giving. This sacrificial giving is the basis of Christian stewardship as we worship God through gratitude and offering. This woman didn't give much, yet she gave everything. It's not the monetary value that's significant—it's the position of her heart.

> [41] And he sat down opposite the treasury and watched the people putting money into the offering box. Many rich people put in large sums. [42] And a poor widow came and put in two small copper coins, which make a penny. [43] And he called his disciples to him and said to them, "Truly, I say to you, this poor widow has put in more than all those who are contributing to the offering box. [44] For they all contributed out of their abundance, but she out of her poverty has put in everything she had, all she had to live on."
>
> MARK 12:41-44

4. This is what Paul wanted to point out in Philippians 4:17. He says, essentially, "It's not about the gift—it's about the fruit." What do you think he means by this?

_____

_____

_____

_____

We find this concept of fruit throughout the Bible, and one of the most well-known passages about it is in another of Paul's letters, this one to the Galatians. As we read these verses, notice how each virtue is separated with a cause and effect. Paul is not simply telling us about abstract concepts—he's speaking about actual, actionable outcome.

> But the fruit produced by the Holy Spirit within you is
> divine love in all its varied expressions:
>> joy that overflows,
>> peace that subdues,
>> patience that endures,
>> kindness in action,
>> a life full of virtue,
>> faith that prevails,
>> gentleness of heart, and
>> strength of spirit.
>> Never set the law above these qualities, for they are meant
> to be limitless.
>
> GALATIANS 5:22-23, TPT

Fruit trees aren't large in stature. They're not giant redwoods. And they're not as wide as an enormous Montezuma cypress dubbed "árbol del Tule" (whose trunk diameter is almost as long as an NBA-sized basketball court!).[13] Fruit trees are unassuming. In fact, if fruit trees didn't bear fruit, you likely wouldn't even pay them any notice.

Most of us are also unassuming. And that means we're not much to look at without fruit. Fruit is what draws others to our lives. Fruit is our beauty.

When we live for what really matters, our fruit is healthy and authentic. No fake, plastic fruit here! We're not to be more interested in looking good than actually *being* good.[14] Jesus Himself warned against this:

> You also outwardly appear righteous to others, but within
> you are full of hypocrisy and lawlessness.
>
> MATTHEW 23:28

The quality of the fruit shows the health of the tree. An unhealthy tree cannot produce healthy fruit. But here's the thing: The whole tree needs to be healthy. It's not possible for a single branch to be healthy if the rest of the tree is not healthy. The trunk cannot be in good shape if the roots are unhealthy. In the same way, if we are to produce good and beneficial fruit, our whole life needs to be healthy. If we're praying more yet we're constantly rude to our kids, husband, or roommate, we're not holistically healthy. If we diligently study the Bible and yet look at porn or tear down people with our friends, we're not producing good fruit.

> [Jesus said,] "If you grow a healthy tree, you'll pick healthy fruit. If you grow a diseased tree, you'll pick worm-eaten fruit. The fruit tells you about the tree."
> MATTHEW 12:33, MSG

Fortunately for us, our God is a patient God. Do you remember the parable Jesus told about the barren fig tree?

> ⁶ And he told this parable: "A man had a fig tree planted in his vineyard, and he came seeking fruit on it and found none. ⁷ And he said to the vinedresser, 'Look, for three years now I have come seeking fruit on this fig tree, and I find none. Cut it down. Why should it use up the ground?' ⁸ And he answered him, 'Sir, let it alone this year also, until I dig around it and put on manure. ⁹ Then if it should bear fruit next year, well and good; but if not, you can cut it down.'"
> LUKE 13:6-9

Jesus tells us that we need to fertilize ourselves. We need to cultivate a life that invests in healthy growth. I recently finished Margaret Feinberg's beautifully written (and hunger inducing) book, *Taste and See: Discovering God Among Butchers, Bakers, and Fresh Food Makers.*

In one chapter, she shares about what she learned while traveling to Madera, California, to visit a fig farm. One of my biggest takeaways from that story (other than the fact that, "once plucked from the tree, a fresh fig has only an eight- to fourteen-day window to be enjoyed,"[15] which is why many grocery stores don't carry them . . . who knew!) is this:

> Spiritual fruit is the result of being rooted in relationship with Christ. Any fruit—including love, joy, peace, patience, kindness, goodness, faithfulness, gentleness, and self-control—provides evidence of the work of the Holy Spirit. As we ground ourselves in God, he plants and weeds, nourishes and fertilizes, prunes and harvests. The yield of our fruitfulness are the qualities that make us look more like him.[16]

5. Where in your life do you sense the need for growth? What are some practical ways you might partner with God's work in that area?

As we seek to grow, the Lord is right there with us, cultivating our lives. He is patient, and He fulfills His promises (2 Peter 3:9). When we have faith that prevails, we produce fruit. When we are kind in action, we produce fruit. And when we serve, we produce fruit.

We don't serve out of our own strength, though. As we learn in 1 Peter 4:11, we need to serve "by the strength that God supplies." When we do that, He is glorified, and we get to live in the fruit of His glory. As a body of believers, we are called to care for others, even when we think we have nothing to give—because we are operating out of God's strength, not our own. We are merely the vessels God wants to use for His glory and the growth of the body of Christ.

The Philippian church understood this God-equipped service, and Paul's heart is full. He says that he "[has] an abundance" (Philippians 4:18, NASB). We see in the BLB that this word *perisseuō* (περισσεύω, pronounced *peh-rees-syoo-oh*) means "to . . . overflow," "to have in abundance," "to excel"—and my favorite description: "to superabound."[17]

Paul wraps up his letter with a full heart. His friends in Philippi have sent a helper (Epaphroditus); they've sent a gift that helps his survival and well-being. They've encouraged him; they are listening to his teaching and implementing his direction. He feels heard, he feels supported, he feels loved. Because Paul understands that his suffering from prison is temporal, he's able to swim in the love and care from his friends. With this, how could he *not* feel like his cup runneth over?

Ask God what fruit He wants to cultivate in your life. Where does He want you to serve Him as you serve those around you?

Amen.

WEEK 7 • *Day 4*

 READ PHILIPPIANS 4:17-20

When we flew into being a family of eight, bringing an infant and a teenager into our family at the same time, I was drowning in overwhelm. A woman I barely knew, a mom of young kids herself, reached out to me and asked if she could bring dinner. Of course I said yes, excited that I didn't have to think of a meal for an evening— but when she showed up, she brought unexpected abundance. She carried in bags and bags of food. One bag was full of our dinner (and dessert . . . thank you, Jesus). Another was full of easy breakfasts, and yet another held food the kids could easily pack into their own lunch-boxes for school. I was overwhelmed with gratitude. We're friends to this day. This woman was more of a blessing than she'll ever fully comprehend.

I love how *The Message* translates this second portion of Philippians 4:17: "I do want you to experience the blessing that issues from generosity."

And that's really what it is, isn't it? There is blessing in being a bless-ing. If we are to be like Jesus, we need to serve others and be generous and charitable, doing things without expecting anything in return:

> For even the Son of Man came not to be served but to serve, and to give his life as a ransom for many.
>
> MARK 10:45

1. Have you ever experienced blessing in being a blessing? What did God teach you through that experience?

Not only does Paul say the Philippians will be blessed through their generosity, but also that God will supply every one of their needs.

> [18] I have received full payment, and more. I am well supplied, having received from Epaphroditus the gifts you sent, a fragrant offering, a sacrifice acceptable and pleasing to God. [19] And my God will supply every need of yours according to his riches in glory in Christ Jesus. [20] To our God and Father be glory forever and ever. Amen.
>
> PHILIPPIANS 4:18-20

Paul's needs are met because the Philippian church is acting on behalf of the Lord Jesus Christ. They're showing how the church (and every believer) should love.

2. Look again at Philippians 4:19-20. What exactly is *glory*? Use the BLB to dig in.

_____

_____

_____

_____

_____

_____

_____

_____

_____

The word used for *glory* here in Philippians 4:20 is *doxa* (δόξα, pronounced *dok-sah*), which means "always a good opinion concerning someone, resulting in praise, honour, and glory" and "worship."[18] And if you're wondering if *doxology* stemmed from this word, you're spot on!

History Lesson

When I was pregnant with our first, Ben and I considered naming him Dox, after the term describing a short hymn of praise to the Lord (I still think it would have been cool). This Greek word *doxa*, though, means "common belief or popular opinion." In fact, our English words *orthodoxy* and *heterodoxy* both come from this ancient word. However, between the third and first centuries BC, when the Septuagint was written, the word *doxa* acquired new meaning.[19]

The Septuagint is a translation of the Hebrew Scriptures into Greek by seventy-two Hebrew scholars in Alexandria. During this translation, the scholars interpreted the Hebrew word for glory as *doxa*.[20] The Septuagint translation of the Hebrew Scriptures was what the early church used, and it is quoted frequently by the authors of the New Testament.

The word *doxology* means a study of praise, but many dictionaries define the term as an expression of praise to God (typically offered through song). Both liturgical Protestant churches and the Catholic church have doxologies.[21]

The term *doxology* is not found in the Bible, but the topics used in doxologies are certainly scriptural. Examples of this include praising God for His blessings (Ephesians 1:3), ascribing to Him all glory (Romans 11:36; Ephesians 3:21), and declaring the truth of the Trinity (Matthew 28:19).

What would it sound like for you to glorify the Lord through song? I grew up in a beautiful church with carved wooden pews and a grand pipe organ. When I was in high school, I began attending the more contemporary service in the gym. But though I don't tend to worship with hymns anymore, they hold a very special place in my heart. Maybe they do for you, too. This doxology has always been one of my favorites:

Praise God, from whom all blessings flow;
Praise him, all creatures here below;
Praise him above, ye heavenly host:
Praise Father, Son, and Holy Ghost.[22]

 Pen down your own doxology of praise to God as we wrap up our time today:

_____

_____

_____

_____

_____

_____

_____

_____

_____

_____

Amen.

WEEK 7 • *Day 5*

READ PHILIPPIANS 4:21-23

One of my best friends is working really hard to live a life of unity: unity with Christ and unity among survivors. Crystal is a Columbine survivor. And when I say survivor, I mean she was in the library that day. If you remember anything about that painful day, you'll know that the library was the place with the most tragedy of all. She was one of the few who sneaked out unscathed in body, but she is forever changed in spirit. Crystal now travels all over the world when a mass catastrophe erupts. In fact, she's one of the first to board a plane straight for the eye of the storm to love on and bring the light of Jesus to others who will also be changed forever. The Lord never wastes any experiences, even devastatingly tragic ones (*especially* devastatingly tragic ones!)—and what Satan meant for destruction, God is using to bring life. Recently Crystal and several survivors from other mass tragedies have joined forces with the incredible folks at The Onsite Foundation in Nashville and are providing trauma-informed therapy and educational tools and resources for other survivors to help heal. The curriculum is called "Triumph Over Tragedy."

To me, this is the ultimate form of unity and community: bringing people together from varying walks of life, varying ages and ethnicities, and even varying belief systems with the sole intent to love on them and help guide them toward restoration. I think Paul would smile at this, don't you?

Paul's final words today sum up his call to the life that matters. As he moves into a conclusion and benediction, he reminds the Philippians to greet every believer.

1. The word *greet* or *aspazomai* (ἀσπάζομαι, pronounced *ah-spad-zo-mai*) is used here three times in two short verses. What does it mean?

2. Why do you think Paul was so intentional and specific in ending his letter to Philippi with this command and encouragement?

We know from reading the entirety of this letter that unity within the church (i.e., believers, not a brick-and-mortar church building) is paramount. Sharing love and embracing unity is truly the basis of what both Jesus and Paul want us to learn as we live for what really matters. By asking the Philippians to "greet every saint in Christ Jesus," he's essentially saying, "Put your differences aside, drawing yourself to other believers and receiving them with joy and welcoming arms."

Bob Goff sums this up perfectly:

> Jesus talked to His friends a lot about how we should identify ourselves. He said it wouldn't be what we said we believed or all the good we hoped to do someday. Nope, He said we would identify ourselves simply by how we loved people. It's tempting to think there is more to it, but there's not. Love isn't something we fall into; love is someone we become.[23]

Paul's request and command reminds us how easily we are pulled apart by differences in doctrine, denomination, politics, music, preaching style, and so many other things. We all love one God and are called to love Him first and others second. Our own interests come after those things. Paul wants this to stay at the forefront of our minds so we can come together as one body, not small groups operating separately toward the same goal. I love how J. A. Motyer explains it for our lives today: "We have allowed the church to lose its distinctiveness. . . . We have lost the unity without which a resolute stand is impossible."[24]

3. What are some tangible, practical ways you can help form unity among believers so we can stand together as we live for the gospel and make a difference in the world for God's Kingdom?

Unity means living out the Good News of Jesus in the world around us. Yes, we uphold the truth of God's Word, but it should push us to live out what it's *for*—not be known for sitting back and being against things.

4. Based on his letter to the Philippians and everything we've learned about him from the rest of Scripture, what is Paul *for*?

When I reflect on Paul's priorities in the book of Philippians, I think of a song my mom used to sing to my brother Erik and me when we were growing up: "We are one in the Spirit, we are one in the Lord . . ."[25] These words come from Jesus' words to His disciples in John 13:34-35. Let's bury this truth deep inside our own hearts:

Let me give you a new command: Love one another. In the same way I loved you, you love one another. This is how everyone will recognize that you are my disciples—when they see the love you have for each other.

MSG

5. What's another word for disciple? Circle all that apply.

follower   believer   learner   convert

devotee   enthusiast   freak

You should have circled every single one.[26] (Yes, even freak—you should probably just embrace being a Jesus freak at this point!) Jesus gave this command to His twelve disciples, but every one of us who follows Jesus is also a disciple. That means His command is for you and me too.

Jesus doesn't say to love the ones who seem like they're making good decisions. He doesn't say love only those who have the same faith beliefs as you or agree with you politically. Jesus gives us a command, and that command is that we love all people.

Even the unlovable. Even those who think differently. Even those who have hurt us. Even those who rub us the wrong way.

We must be unified in our love toward all . . . because this is how we show Jesus to others. You, dear friend, may be the only example of Jesus someone ever sees.

6. In the four chapters we've studied together, Paul has given us a glimpse of the Philippians as part of the body of Christ. What have these believers taught us about living for what really matters?

_____

_____

_____

_____

_____

_____

Paul has talked about the needs of the Philippian church, as well as our own. He's discussed their successes, their responsibilities, and the dangers they need to face head on. He's highlighted how they've loved well and how they could grow in unity. Through Paul's words, we learn how God wants to use us in our own lives and within our own body of believers today.

As we wrap up our time together, heed Paul's words to greet one another warmly, to live in unity and not get caught up in the minutiae that ultimately distracts from our goal of living for Him and His glory. We are to show that we are different, that we know how to love because we've learned from the One who created love. Let's join together and live for what really matters:

> Summing it all up, friends, I'd say you'll do best by filling your minds and meditating on things true, noble, reputable, authentic, compelling, gracious—the best, not the worst; the beautiful, not the ugly; things to praise, not things to curse. Put into practice what you learned from me, what you heard and saw and realized. Do that, and God, who makes everything work together, will work you into his most excellent harmonies.
>
> PHILIPPIANS 4:8-9, MSG

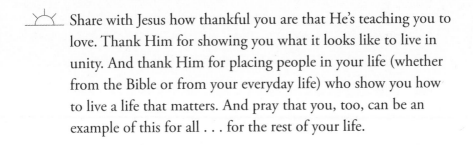 Share with Jesus how thankful you are that He's teaching you to love. Thank Him for showing you what it looks like to live in unity. And thank Him for placing people in your life (whether from the Bible or from your everyday life) who show you how to live a life that matters. And pray that you, too, can be an example of this for all . . . for the rest of your life.

Amen.

WEEK 7 • *Notes*

Share your biggest takeaways from this week:

Acknowledgments

Jesus: You're funny. I never, ever would have thought I'd write Bible studies. But the other day when I asked You, "Why did I waste so much time on an art history degree if that wasn't even the plan?"—remember what You whispered to my heart? *Nothing is wasted. You now study the Bible exactly the way you learned to study art—digging into culture, society, politics, and everything in between—except now you're doing it to figure out what inspired Me to include each story, parable, psalm, person, or tiniest little detail.*

No experience is ever wasted. I pray, Lord Jesus, that none of me is wasted either.

Benny: Thank you for helping push me out of bed each morning so I have time to write, study, and spend time with Jesus before the kids wake. Thank you for taking them on fun "daddy dates" on some evenings and weekends so I can do that some more. Thank you for being my sounding board, my encourager when I thought, *Who am I to do this?*, and the love of my life. I am so overwhelmingly in love with you.

Momma and Daddy: Thank you for creating a home in which I saw both of you read and study Scripture. Daddy, you and your color-coded, highlighted pages—and Momma, you at the dining table, workbooks and Bible spread in front of you on warm days . . . and on the floor next to the heating vent when it was cold. Thank you for being living examples to me.

Elsabet, Imani, Laith, Anton, Ezekiel, and Abreham: I have no idea if you'll ever sit down and do the studies I write, but I do pray that Jesus captivates you the same way He does me. I pray that seeing me constantly pour over Scripture lights a fire in you, too. Loves, *dive in.* Don't live on what others regurgitate to you about God's Word . . . figure it out yourself. See and learn about Jesus yourself. If you ever don't know where to start, ask Jesus. He'll teach you. He is, after all, the original Teacher. I love every one of you and am so proud to be your mom. XO

Kiesha Yokers: Thank you for loving and encouraging me well. I've never met anyone who makes me laugh harder and yet challenges and encourages me so deeply. I love you, girl.

Nirup Alphonse: This is all your fault. Thank you for . . . *challenging me? telling me? ordering me?* to stop leading Bible studies that I've purchased and instead write them myself. Thank you for telling me I really could do this. Thanks for believing in me, dear friend.

Jana Burson: Thank you for taking a chance on me in so many ways. And thank you for being the type of agent who isn't just about business but loves on me well. You're amazing.

Don Pape: I'm still pinching myself that you believed in me enough to sign me for three studies. Not only that, but for standing with me while sharing that we need to "skate to where the puck is going to be, not where it has been" (Wayne Gretzky). You're a true visionary. Thank you for your emails and texts saying you're praying for me and for taking us all out to fun dinners because I'm not just your author, I'm family.

Caitlyn Carlson: Who'd have known a cup of coffee to talk about my proposal would lead to acquiring not only three books but also a deep friendship?! The BEST. Thank you for both pushing and having grace with me as you edited my one billion words. I adore you, girl.

Elizabeth Schroll, Olivia Eldredge, and Dave Zimmerman: Thank you for sharing your editorial giftings, your granola bars, your dried mango, and your jumper cables. You are amazing friends and fantastic talents. Thanks for loving me well. (PS—When can we go back to that Thai place?)

David Geeslin, Madeline Daniels, Isabella Cortes, Linda Schmitt, Adam Graber, and Libby Dykstra: I'm overwhelmed to have not only the incredible team over at NavPress but you at Tyndale, too. You, dear friends, heard me. I had a vision and you caught my excitement, even though it's not necessarily "the way things are done." Thank you for jumping in and sharing the message of Jesus in the way I felt Him asking me to. I've enjoyed every second.

Creighton Petro: I love that one day I'm walking into Chauncy's office, meeting her for the first time, and the next day she tells me, "You have to meet my husband." (Chauncy, you were SO right.) Thank you for believing in me enough to jump on board with *Let's Party Like Girls* first and now all the video fun for our Get Wisdom series. I hope this is just the beginning!

Appendix

If you're new to Bible commentaries or want to expand your reference library, I recommend the following options.

GENERAL BIBLE COMMENTARIES

FULL BIBLE

Henry, Matthew. *Matthew Henry's Concise Commentary of the Whole Bible*. Nashville: Thomas Nelson, 2003.

Wenham, G. J., et al., eds. *New Bible Commentary*, 21st-century ed. Downers Grove, IL: InterVarsity Press, 1994.

OLD TESTAMENT

Goldstein, Elyse, ed. *The Women's Torah Commentary: New Insights from Women Rabbis on the 54 Weekly Torah Portions*. Woodstock, VT: Jewish Lights, 2000.

Walton, John H., Victor H. Matthews, and Mark W. Chavalas. *IVP Bible Background Commentary: Old Testament*. Downers Grove, IL: IVP Academic, 2000.

NEW TESTAMENT

Keener, Craig S. *IVP Bible Background Commentary: New Testament*. Downers Grove, IL: IVP Academic, 2014.

COMMENTARIES ON PHILIPPIANS

Getz, Gene A. *Paul: Living for the Call of Christ*. Men of Character series. Nashville: Broadman & Holman, 2000.

Martin, Ralph P. *Philippians: An Introduction and Commentary*. Tyndale New Testament Commentaries, vol. 11. Downers Grove, IL: IVP Academic, 1987.

Motyer, J. A. *The Message of Philippians: Jesus Our Joy*. The Bible Speaks Today. Downers Grove, IL: InterVarsity Press, 1984.

Piper, John. *Why I Love the Apostle Paul: 30 Reasons*. Wheaton, IL: Crossway, 2019.

Thielman, Frank. *Philippians: The NIV Application Commentary.* Grand Rapids, MI: Zondervan, 1995.

ADDITIONAL RESOURCES

APPS

Bible Gateway (or biblegateway.com)
Bible Hub (or biblehub.com)
Bible Study Tools (or biblestudytools.com)
Blue Letter Bible (or blueletterbible.org)
YouVersion (or youversion.com)

BIBLE DICTIONARY

Marshall, I. Howard, et al., eds. *New Bible Dictionary*, 3rd ed. Leicester, England: InterVarsity Press, 2004.

BIBLE HISTORY

Bright, John. *A History of Israel.* 4th ed. Louisville, KY: Westminster John Knox, 2000.

BIBLICAL MAPS

Isbouts, Jean-Pierre. *The Biblical World: An Illustrated Atlas.* Washington, DC: National Geographic, 2007.
Rose Book of Bible Charts, Maps, and Time Lines. Torrance, CA: Rose Publishing, 2015.

Notes

INTRODUCTION

1. Please see the appendix.

WEEK 1: LIVING IN AUTHENTICITY

1. See Acts 9:4–13:9 (headings were excluded from this count).
2. Bible Hub, "3972. Paulos," accessed January 16, 2020, https://biblehub.com
/greek/3972.htm.
3. Blue Letter Bible, "Lexicon: Strong's G2537—*kainos*," accessed December 20, 2019,
https://www.blueletterbible.org/lang/lexicon/lexicon.cfm?Strongs=G2537&t=ESV.
4. Melissa Petruzzello, "St. Paul's Contributions to the New Testament," accessed
December 29, 2019, https://www.britannica.com/list/st-pauls-contributions
-to-the-new-testament.
5. Blue Letter Bible, "Lexicon: Strong's G4632—*skeuos*," accessed December 29, 2019,
https://www.blueletterbible.org/lang/lexicon/lexicon.cfm?Strongs=G4632&t=ESV.
6. John Piper, *Why I Love the Apostle Paul: 30 Reasons* (Wheaton, IL: Crossway, 2019),
introduction.
7. David Spell, *Peter and Paul in Acts* (Eugene, OR: Wipf & Stock, 2006), 125.
8. Stanley J. Grenz and Denise Muir Kjesbo, *Women in the Church: A Biblical Theology
of Women in Ministry* (Downers Grove, IL: InterVarsity Press, 1995), 78.
9. Blue Letter Bible, "Lexicon: Strong's G2967—*kōlyō*," accessed December 30, 2019,
https://www.blueletterbible.org/lang/lexicon/lexicon.cfm?Strongs=G2967&t=ESV.
10. Mark Cartwright, "Philippi," Ancient History Encyclopedia, May 4, 2016, https://
www.ancient.eu/Philippi/.
11. Mark Cartwright, "Tyrian Purple," Ancient History Encyclopedia, July 21, 2016,
https://www.ancient.eu/Tyrian_Purple/; and E. J. Banks, "Thyatira," Bible Study
Tools, accessed January 16, 2020, https://www.biblestudytools.com/encyclopedias
/isbe/thyatira.html.
12. Christy Cobb, *Slavery, Gender, Truth, and Power in Luke–Acts and Other Ancient
Narratives* (Cham, Switzerland: Palgrave MacMillan, 2019), 174.
13. Blue Letter Bible, "Lexicon: Strong's G3586—*xylon*," accessed December 30, 2019,
https://www.blueletterbible.org/lang/lexicon/lexicon.cfm?Strongs=G3586&t=ESV.

14. Margaret Shepherd, *The Art of the Handwritten Note: A Guide to Reclaiming Civilized Communications* (New York: Broadway Books, 2002).

15. "Where the 'Christian' Name Really Came From," *Relevant*, April 8, 2013, https://relevantmagazine.com/god/where-christian-name-really-came/.

16. Blue Letter Bible, "Lexicon: Strong's G4862—*syn*," accessed December 30, 2019, https://www.blueletterbible.org/lang/lexicon/lexicon.cfm?Strongs=G4862&t=ESV.

17. Blue Letter Bible, "Lexicon: Strong's G2168—*eucharisteō*," accessed December 30, 2019, https://www.blueletterbible.org/lang/lexicon/lexicon.cfm?Strongs=G2168&t=ESV.

18. Ann Voskamp, *One Thousand Gifts Devotional: Reflections on Finding Everyday Graces* (Grand Rapids, MI: Zondervan, 2012), day 48.

19. Adapted from ESV.

20. Donald Miller, *Scary Close: Dropping the Act and Finding True Intimacy* (Nashville: Nelson Books, 2014), 12.

21. Blue Letter Bible, "Lexicon: Strong's G1922—*epignōsis*," accessed December 30, 2019, https://www.blueletterbible.org/lang/lexicon/lexicon.cfm?Strongs=G1922&t=ESV.

22. Blue Letter Bible, "Lexicon: Strong's G 1381—*dokimazō*," accessed January 16, 2020, https://www.blueletterbible.org/lang/lexicon/lexicon.cfm?Strongs=G1381&t=ESV.

23. Ralph P. Martin, *Philippians: An Introduction and Commentary*, Tyndale New Testament Commentaries, vol. 11 (Downers Grove, IL: IVP Academic, 1987), 72.

24. See the *Interlinear* for Philippians 1:10.

25. Frank Thielman, *Philippians: The NIV Application Commentary* (Grand Rapids, MI: Zondervan, 1995), 41.

WEEK 2: CHOOSING JOY

1. To learn more about the significance of Paul's Roman citizenship, see Stephanie Hertzenberg, "Why Does the Bible Specify That Paul Was a Roman Citizen?," Beliefnet, https://www.beliefnet.com/faiths/christianity/why-does-the-bible-specify-that-paul-was-a-roman-citizen.aspx.

2. John MacArthur, *The New Testament Commentary: Philippians* (Chicago: Moody, 2001), 60.

3. To view a map of Paul's route, see "Paul's First Missionary Journey Map," Conforming to Jesus Ministry, https://www.conformingtojesus.com/charts-maps/en/paul%27s_first_journey_map.htm.

4. To view a map of Paul's route, see "Paul's Second Missionary Journey Map," Conforming to Jesus Ministry, https://www.conformingtojesus.com/charts-maps/en/paul's_second_journey_map.htm.

5. To view a map of Paul's route, see "Paul's Third Missionary Journey Map," Conforming to Jesus Ministry, https://www.conformingtojesus.com/images/webpages/pauls_third_missionary_journey1.jpeg.

6. Evan Andrews, "8 Things You May Not Know About the Praetorian Guard," History .com, updated August 29, 2018, https://www.history.com/news/8-things-you-may-not-know-about-the-praetorian-guard.

7. MacArthur, *New Testament Commentary: Philippians*, 60.

8. Adapted from MSG.

9. Bible Hub, "2052. eritheia," accessed January 16, 2020, https://biblehub.com/greek/2052.htm.

10. From Claudia Tate, "Maya Angelou: An Interview," in *Maya Angelou's I Know Why the Caged Bird Sings: A Casebook*, ed. Joanne M. Braxton (New York: Oxford University Press, 1999), 154.

11. *Friday Night Lights* (Universal City, CA: Universal Studios, 2005), DVD.

12. Eddie Kaufholz, "I'm a Christian. Why Am I Still So Scared of Dying?" *Relevant*, November 26, 2014, https://relevantmagazine.com/god/im-christian-why-am-i-still-so-scared-dying/.

13. John Piper, "How Do I Overcome My Fear of Death?" Desiring God, June 6, 2018, https://www.desiringgod.org/interviews/how-do-i-overcome-my-fear-of-death.

14. Blue Letter Bible, "Lexicon: Strong's G2198—*zaō*," accessed December 31, 2019, https://www.blueletterbible.org/lang/lexicon/lexicon.cfm?Strongs=G2198&t=ESV.

15. Lysa TerKeurst, *It's Not Supposed to Be This Way: Finding Unexpected Strength When Disappointments Leave You Shattered* (Nashville: Thomas Nelson, 2018), 45.

16. John Piper, *Why I Love the Apostle Paul: 30 Reasons* (Wheaton, IL: Crossway, 2019), chap. 3.

17. The following chart was inspired by a Pinterest post I saw years ago.

18. Shauna Niequist, *Bittersweet: Thoughts on Change, Grace, and Learning the Hard Way* (Grand Rapids, MI: Zondervan, 2010), 17.

19. Blue Letter Bible, "Lexicon: Strong's G1961—*epimenō*," accessed December 31, 2019, https://www.blueletterbible.org/lang/lexicon/lexicon.cfm?Strongs=G1961&t=ESV.

WEEK 3: LIVING LIKE JESUS

1. Bob Goff, *Everybody Always: Becoming Love in a World Full of Setbacks and Difficult People* (Nashville: Nelson Books, 2018), 4.

2. Blue Letter Bible, "Lexicon: Strong's G4739—*stēkō*," accessed December 31, 2019, https://www.blueletterbible.org/lang/lexicon/lexicon.cfm?Strongs=G4739&t=ESV.

3. Blue Letter Bible, "Lexicon: Strong's G4739—*stēkō*," accessed December 31, 2019, https://www.blueletterbible.org/lang/lexicon/lexicon.cfm?Strongs=G4739&t=ESV.

4. Blue Letter Bible, "Lexicon: Strong's G2758—*kenoō*," accessed January 2, 2020, https://www.blueletterbible.org/lang/lexicon/lexicon.cfm?Strongs=G2758&t=ESV.

5. Calvin, quoted in J. A. Motyer, *The Message of Philippians: Jesus Our Joy* (Downers Grove, IL: InterVarsity Press, 1984), 113.

6. John Dart, "Up Against Caesar," Society of Biblical Literature, accessed January 17, 2020, https://www.sbl-site.org/publications/article.aspx?ArticleId=388.

7. Lynn H. Cohick, *Philippians*, The Story of God Bible Commentary (Grand Rapids, MI: Zondervan, 2013), chap. 7.

8. Blue Letter Bible, "Lexicon: Strong's G3842—*pantote*," accessed January 2, 2020, https://www.blueletterbible.org/lang/lexicon/lexicon.cfm?Strongs=G3842&t=ESV.

WEEK 4: RISING UP

1. Richard N. Longenecker, *The Expositor's Bible Commentary: Acts* (Grand Rapids, MI: Zondervan, 1995), 227–228.

2. John B. Polhill, *Paul and His Letters* (Nashville: B & H Academic, 1999), 92.

3. Study Light, "Bible Commentaries: Expository Notes of Dr. Thomas Constable: Acts 14," accessed January 16, 2020, https://www.studylight.org/commentaries/dcc/acts-14.html.

4. Blue Letter Bible, "Lexicon: Strong's G242—*hallomai*," accessed January 2, 2020, https://www.blueletterbible.org/lang/lexicon/lexicon.cfm?Strongs=G242&t=ESV.

5. W. F. Boyd, "Lois," in James Hastings, ed., *Dictionary of the Apostolic Church*, vol. I, Aaron–Lystra (New York: Charles Scribner's Sons, 1916), 704.

6. Philip Nel, *Dr. Seuss: American Icon* (New York: Continuum, 2005), 32.

7. Blue Letter Bible, "Lexicon: Strong's G3309—*merimnaō*," accessed January 2, 2020, https://www.blueletterbible.org/lang/lexicon/lexicon.cfm?Strongs=G3309&t=ESV.

8. Bob Goff, *Everybody Always* (Nashville: Nelson Books, 2018), 43.

9. Google, "synergy," accessed January 16, 2020, https://www.google.com/search?q=synergy&oq=synergy&aqs=chrome..69i57j0l6j69i60.830j0j4&sourceid=chrome&ie=UTF-8.

10. Blue Letter Bible, "Lexicon: Strong's G4961—*systratiōtēs*," accessed January 2, 2020, https://www.blueletterbible.org/lang/lexicon/lexicon.cfm?Strongs=G4961&t=ESV.

11. Blue Letter Bible, "Lexicon: Strong's G652—*apostolos*," accessed January 2, 2020, https://www.blueletterbible.org/lang/lexicon/lexicon.cfm?Strongs=G652&t=ESV.

12. Blue Letter Bible, "Lexicon: Strong's G3011—*leitourgos*," accessed January 3, 2020, https://www.blueletterbible.org/lang/lexicon/lexicon.cfm?Strongs=G3011&t=ESV.

13. Blue Letter Bible, "Lexicon: Strong's G3985—*peirazō*," accessed January 3, 2020, https://www.blueletterbible.org/lang/lexicon/lexicon.cfm?Strongs=G3985&t=ESV.

14. As quoted in *The Holman Student Bible* (Nashville: Holman Bible Publishers, 2007), 1650.

WEEK 5: WATCH AND LEARN

1. Blue Letter Bible, "Lexicon: Strong's G3062—*loipos*," accessed January 3, 2020, https://www.blueletterbible.org/lang/lexicon/lexicon.cfm?Strongs=G3062&t=ESV.

2. *ESV Study Bible* (Wheaton, IL: Crossway, 2008), 2285.

3. To read more about this first-century controversy about circumcision, see Oskar Skarsaune, *In the Shadow of the Temple: Jewish Influences on Early Christianity* (Downers Grove, IL: InterVarsity Press, 2002), chap. 8.

4. "The Rules of the Pharisees," PursueGod.org, accessed January 3, 2020, https://www.pursuegod.org/rules-pharisees/.

5. All credit to Brené Brown for this gut-punch description! Brené Brown, *The Gifts of Imperfection: Let Go of Who You Think You're Supposed to Be and Embrace Who You Are* (Center City, MN: Hazeldon, 2010), 37.

6. Amanda Jenkins, *Confessions of a Raging Perfectionist: Learning to Be Free* (Carol Stream, IL: Tyndale, 2013), 25.

7. Jenkins, *Confessions*, xii.

8. Jenkins, *Confessions*, xii.

9. Thank you to Nirup Alphonse for helping me express this idea more clearly.

10. Blue Letter Bible, "Lexicon: Strong's G5046—*teleios*," accessed January 3, 2020, https://www.blueletterbible.org/lang/lexicon/lexicon.cfm?Strongs=G5046&t=NASB.

11. Blue Letter Bible, "Lexicon: Strong's G2799—*klaiō*," accessed January 3, 2020, https://www.blueletterbible.org/lang/lexicon/lexicon.cfm?Strongs=G2799&t=ESV.

12. "Which Animals Does the Bible Designate as 'Clean' and 'Unclean'?," Beyond Today, accessed January 3, 2020, https://www.ucg.org/bible-study-tools/booklets/what-does-the-bible-teach-about-clean-and-unclean-meats/infographic-which.

13. Blue Letter Bible, "Lexicon: Strong's G2836—*koilia*," accessed January 3, 2020, https://www.blueletterbible.org/lang/lexicon/lexicon.cfm?Strongs=G2836&t=ESV.

14. Ralph P. Martin, *Philippians*, Tyndale New Testament Commentaries, vol. 11 (Downers Grove, IL: IVP Academic, 1987), 165.

WEEK 6: LIVE THE EXAMPLE

1. Blue Letter Bible, "Lexicon: Strong's G5426—*phroneō*," accessed January 3, 2020, https://www.blueletterbible.org/lang/lexicon/lexicon.cfm?Strongs=G5426&t=ESV.

2. John Rutherfurd, "Yoke-fellow," Bible Study Tools, accessed January 3, 2020, https://www.biblestudytools.com/encyclopedias/isbe/yoke-fellow.html.

3. Blue Letter Bible, "Lexicon: Strong's G4805—*syzygos*," accessed January 3, 2020, https://www.blueletterbible.org/lang/lexicon/lexicon.cfm?Strongs=G4805&t=ESV.

4. Ralph P. Martin, *Philippians*, Tyndale New Testament Commentaries, vol. 11 (Downers Grove, IL: IVP Academic, 1987), 173.

5. J. A. Motyer, *The Message of Philippians* (Downers Grove, IL: InterVarsity Press, 1984), 203.

6. "What's the Difference between Joy and Happiness?," Compassion International, accessed December 29, 2019, https://www.compassion.com/sponsor_a_child/difference-between-joy-and-happiness.htm.

7. Blue Letter Bible, "Lexicon: Strong's G5463—*chairō*," accessed January 5, 2020, https://www.blueletterbible.org/lang/lexicon/lexicon.cfm?Strongs=G5463&t=ESV.

8. Blue Letter Bible, "Lexicon: Strong's G1933—*epieikēs*," accessed January 5, 2020, https://www.blueletterbible.org/lang/lexicon/lexicon.cfm?Strongs=G1933&t=ESV.

9. Mark Batterson, *The Circle Maker: Praying Circles around Your Biggest Dreams and Greatest Fears* (Grand Rapids, MI: Zondervan, 2016), 15–16.

10. Blue Letter Bible, "Lexicon: Strong's G3049—*logizomai*," accessed January 5, 2020, https://www.blueletterbible.org/lang/lexicon/lexicon.cfm?Strongs=G3049&t=ESV.

11. Motyer, *Message of Philippians*, 212.

12. "Peace-Shalom (Hebrew Word Study)," Precept Austin, March 21, 2019, https://www.preceptaustin.org/shalom_-_definition.

13. Blue Letter Bible, "Lexicon: Strong's H7965—*shalowm*," accessed January 5, 2020, https://www.blueletterbible.org/lang/lexicon/lexicon.cfm?Strongs=H7965&t=ESV.

14. Encyclopædia Britannica, s.v. "Hebrew Language," accessed January 5, 2020, https://www.britannica.com/topic/Hebrew-language.

WEEK 7: THE LORD'S PROVISION

1. Blue Letter Bible, "Lexicon: Strong's G842—*autarkēs*," accessed January 5, 2020, https://www.blueletterbible.org/lang/lexicon/lexicon.cfm?Strongs=G842&t=ESV.

2. John Piper, *Future Grace: The Purifying Power of the Promises of God*, rev. ed. (Colorado Springs: Multnomah, 2012), 224.

3. "What to Do When 'Community over Competition' Gets Complicated with Natalie Frankie," *The Mary Marantz Show*, September 4, 2019, podcast, http://marymarantz.libsyn.com/what-to-do-when-community-over-competition-gets-complicated-with-natalie-franke.

4. "What to Do When 'Community Over Competition' Gets Complicated."

5. J. A. Motyer, *The Message of Philippians* (Downers Grove, IL: InterVarsity Press, 1984), 220.

6. Blue Letter Bible, "Lexicon: Strong's H5797—'*oz*," accessed January 6, 2020, https://www.blueletterbible.org/lang/lexicon/lexicon.cfm?Strongs=H5797&t=ESV.

7. Blue Letter Bible, "Lexicon: Strong's G4790—*sygkoinōneō*," accessed January 6, 2020, https://www.blueletterbible.org/lang/lexicon/lexicon.cfm?Strongs=G4790&t=ESV.

8. Blue Letter Bible, "Lexicon: Strong's G4862—*syn*," accessed January 6, 2020, https://www.blueletterbible.org/lang/lexicon/lexicon.cfm?strongs=G4862&t=ESV.

9. Bible Tools, "Greek/Hebrew Definitions," accessed January 16, 2020, https://www.bibletools.org/index.cfm/fuseaction/Lexicon.show/ID/G2842/koinonia.htm.

10. David Mathis, *Habits of Grace: Enjoying Jesus through the Spiritual Disciplines* (Wheaton, IL: Crossway, 2016), 145–146.

11. Blue Letter Bible, "Lexicon: Strong's G2347—*thlipsis*," accessed January 6, 2020, https://www.blueletterbible.org/lang/lexicon/lexicon.cfm?Strongs=G2347&t=ESV.

12. Ian Morgan Cron and Suzanne Stabile, *The Road Back to You: An Enneagram Journey to Self-Discovery* (Downers Grove, IL: IVP Books, 2016), 125.

13. "General Sherman, the Biggest Tree in the World," Monumental Trees, accessed January 6, 2020, https://www.monumentaltrees.com/en/trees/giantsequoia/biggest_tree_in_the_world/.

14. Don Hooser, "A Fruit of the Spirit—Abundant Fresh Fruit," Beyond Today, January 2, 2010, https://www.ucg.org/the-good-news/a-fruit-of-the-spirit-abundant-fresh-fruit-to-serve-god-and-share-with-others.

15. Margaret Feinberg, *Taste and See: Discovering God among Butchers, Bakers, and Fresh Food Makers* (Grand Rapids, MI: Zondervan, 2019), 57.

16. Feinberg, *Taste and See*, 65.

17. Blue Letter Bible, "Lexicon: Strong's G4052—*perisseuō*," accessed January 6, 2020, https://www.blueletterbible.org/lang/lexicon/lexicon.cfm?Strongs=G4052&t=ESV.

18. Blue Letter Bible, "Lexicon: Strong's G1391—*doxa*," accessed January 6, 2020, https://www.blueletterbible.org/lang/lexicon/lexicon.cfm?Strongs=G1391&t=ESV.

19. Definitions.net, s.v. "Doxa," accessed January 6, 2020, https://www.definitions.net/definition/doxa.

20. Ryan Reeves, "What Is the Septuagint?," Gospel Coalition, August 12, 2018, https://www.thegospelcoalition.org/article/what-is-the-septuagint/.

21. "What Is a Doxology, and Is It Found in the Bible?," Compelling Truth, accessed January 6, 2020, https://www.compellingtruth.org/doxology.html.

22. James D. Smith III, "Where Did We Get the Doxology?," *Christianity Today*, accessed January 17, 2020, https://www.christianitytoday.com/history/issues/issue-31/where-did-we-get-doxology.html.

23. Bob Goff, *Everybody Always* (Nashville: Nelson Books, 2018), 2.

24. J. A. Motyer, *The Message of Philippians: Jesus Our Joy* (Downers Grove, IL: InterVarsity Press, 1984), 224.

25. "They'll Know We Are Christians," lyrics by Peter Scholtes, 1966.

26. Thesaurus.com, s.v. "disciple," accessed January 6, 2020, https://www.thesaurus.com/browse/disciple?s=t.